Also by Patrick Barry

Books

Editing and Advocacy: Volume 1

Good with Words: Speaking and Presenting

Good with Words: Writing and Editing

Notes on Nuance

Punctuation and Persuasion: Volume 1

The Syntax of Sports, Class 1: The Words under the Words

The Syntax of Sports, Class 2: The Power of the Particular

The Syntax of Sports, Class 3: The Rule of Three

The Syntax of Sports, Class 4: Parallel Structure

The Syntax of Sports, Class 5: Rhetorical Repetition

The Syntax of Sports, Class 6: Drafting and Editing

The Syntax of Sports, Class 7: Information Flow

Online Courses

"AI for Lawyers and Other Advocates" (Coursera)

"Feedback Loops: How to Give and Receive High-Quality Feedback" (Coursera)

"Good with Words: Speaking and Presenting" (Coursera)

"Good with Words: Writing and Editing" (Coursera)

Feedback from students and professionals who have taken one of Professor Patrick Barry's AI courses or workshops:

"Take this course! I loved what I learned, and I feel more ready for the future than I did before. It should be required for all law students (and lawyers)."

"I want to thank you for all the time and effort you put into the course. Not only did I enjoy all the in-class lessons and discussions, but this class was the first time I actually liked doing my homework!"

"It was truly a privilege to take this course with Professor Barry. I learned *so* much about AI, society, my peers, and myself."

"I was so impressed by the content and the way you engaged everyone. I meant what I said in front of the room—it is really the first time I have experienced an AI presentation where I felt connected and really curious to explore how I might incorporate parts of AI into my program."

"So many of our survey responses gushed about how great your session was, with one simply exclaiming, 'Professor Barry!'"

"Amazing! One of the best presentations I have ever attended."

"I truly looked forward to every week of class and have now recommended the course to all my friends."

"I wish this course were recorded so I could reexperience it."

AI Tips and Traps

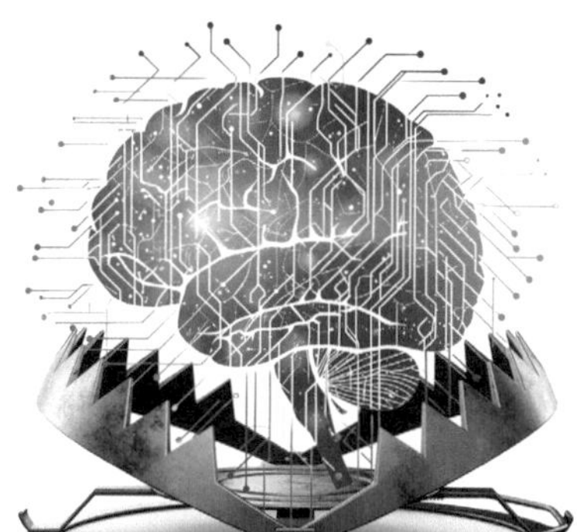

Patrick Barry

Published in the United States of America by
Michigan Publishing
Manufactured in the United States of America

DOI: http://doi.org/10.3998/mpub.13191753

ISBN 978-1-60785-929-1 (paper)
ISBN 978-1-60785-928-4 (open-access)

An imprint of Michigan Publishing, Maize Books serves the publishing needs of the University of Michigan community by making high-quality scholarship widely available in print and online. It represents a new model for authors seeking to share their work within and beyond the academy, offering streamlined selection, production, and distribution processes. Maize Books is intended as a complement to more formal modes of publication in a wide range of disciplinary areas.
http://www.maizebooks.org

For Ethan, whose early support of AI education has produced (1) a lot of learning and (2) a wonderful friendship.

CONTENTS

PART 1
Obstacles and Opportunities

"This [AI technology] gives me joy. It disturbs me. It causes me to lose sleep. It's just a huge kind of mixture of emotions."

—Peter Lee, President of Microsoft Research,
"This American Life: Greetings, People of Earth"

CHAPTER 1
Conspicuously Good

If you do anything with words or language, these next three years are going to be really interesting.

—Steven Johnson, "The Future of AI Is Thrilling, Terrifying, Confusing, and Fascinating"

I have an ambitious goal for us. It is the same one that I have for the students who take the courses on artificial intelligence I teach at the University of Michigan Law School, the University of Chicago Law School, and the UCLA School of Law. By the end of this book—or in my students' case, by the end of the term—I want you to become "conspicuously good" at AI.

I want you to become conspicuously good at using AI. I want you to become conspicuously good at understanding the risks and limitations of AI. And I want you to become conspicuously good at adapting to whatever new AI tools and trends develop in the coming months, years, and decades.

AI Frankfurters

I take the phrase "conspicuously good" from a compliment bestowed on a former justice of the United States Supreme Court, Felix Frankfurter, back when he was a young, 24-year-old prosecutor in New York. His boss at the time, Henry Stimson—who later served in the cabinet of four presidents—described Frankfurter's work as "conspicuously good." What Stimson meant is that Frankfurter's work stood out in a positive way. It attracted laudatory notice and attention.

I want people to say something similar about the work you produce, especially when it comes to AI. I want you to be the person in your office, your industry, or even just your group of friends and family who earns a reputation for being "AI savvy"—someone whom other folks turn to when they need help with an AI-related issue or want to learn more about the latest AI innovation.

Imagine what that kind of status and expertise might do for your job prospects and professional ambitions. Imagine what it might do for your education, as well as your entrepreneurial endeavors—regardless of whether those endeavors are commercial, cultural, or wonderfully idiosyncratic.

More importantly, imagine what being AI savvy might do for your confidence and your own sense that you're equipped to navigate a fast-changing future. As Mhairi Aitken, an ethics fellow at the Alan Turing Institute, playfully observed during a lecture she gave at the Royal Institution in London, it used to be exciting when there was a new AI breakthrough every two to three months. Now it seems like there's one every two to three hours.

Helping students, lawyers, and other advocates adjust to (and then excel in) that kind of fiercely dynamic environment is one of my favorite things about the AI courses and workshops I teach. The participants come from all over the world—India, Japan, Brazil, Nigeria, Mexico, Canada, Australia, France, and Saudi Arabia, not to mention every US state—and I love seeing how, by the end of our time together, their relationship with AI transforms in several positive ways. They become a lot more comfortable with AI. They become a lot more creative with AI. And they each develop a critical eye for spotting what the Princeton computer scientists Arvind Narayanan and Sayash Kapoor call "AI Snake Oil": those bogus, overhyped AI products that "don't work and probably never will." Part of being conspicuously good at AI involves knowing how to avoid what is conspicuously bad.

AI Shock

With that perspective in mind, this book takes a skills-based approach to artificial intelligence. Which tools are worth using? What questions are worth asking? And how do advocates of all kinds continue to add value to clients in a world increasingly populated by chatbots, algorithms, and a wide range of other powerful digital products?

Before engaging with those questions, however, we are going to turn to a somewhat unlikely source: the longtime host of the radio

show and podcast *This American Life*, Ira Glass.

Glass is not a computer scientist. He doesn't work at Google, Microsoft, or Nvidia. Nor is he even a journalist with a special focus on and expertise in technology. But he does have a great ear for useful phrases, and he once built an entire episode of *This American Life* around a phrase that I think may resonate with anybody who has ever felt a bit blindsided by the pace of AI development and the possibility that it will transform everything from the way we work, to the way we learn, to the way we interact.

The phrase is being "unprepared for what has already happened." In the next chapter, we'll explore where it came from.

CHAPTER 2

Unprepared for What Has Already Happened

He found himself lying in the Gallery of Machines . . . his historical neck broken by the sudden eruption of forces totally new.

—Henry Adams, *The Education of Henry Adams* (1907)

The phrase Ira Glass designed an entire episode of *This American Life* around ("unprepared for what has already happened") comes from the journalist Alex Steffen, who used it to capture the unsettling feeling that "the experience and expertise you've built up" may now be obsolete—or at least a lot less valuable.

A good, if dispiriting, example of this feeling appears in the book *Genius Makers: The Mavericks Who Brought AI to Google, Facebook, and the World* by Cade Metz, a technology reporter for *The New York Times*. Metz describes the panic that washed over a veteran researcher at Microsoft named Chris Brockett when Brockett first encountered an artificial intelligence program that could essentially do everything he had spent decades of schooling and professional training learning to do. Physically overcome by the realization that a piece of software had now made his entire skill set and knowledge base irrelevant, Brockett was actually rushed to the hospital because he thought he was having a heart attack. "My fifty-two-year-old body," he later told Metz, "had one of those moments when I saw a future where I wasn't involved."

In *Life 3.0: Being Human in the Age of Artificial Intelligence*, the MIT physicist Max Tegmark expresses a similar worry: "As technology keeps improving, will the rise of AI eventually eclipse those abilities that provide my current sense of self-worth and value on the job market?"

The answer to that question, unnervingly, can often feel outside of our individual control. "We're seeing more AI-related products and advancements in a single day than we saw in a single year a decade ago," a Silicon Valley product manager told a reporter for *Vanity Fair* in 2023. Things have only seemed to accelerate since then.

Even Dario Amodei—the cofounder and CEO of Anthropic, the company that created the popular chatbot Claude—has said he has been a bit shaken, both professionally and personally, by the power of AI tools. For decades, Amodei has been revered as being supersmart (he has a PhD in physics from Princeton) and exceptionally skilled at computer programming (before founding Anthropic, he held high-level positions at Google, Baidu, and OpenAI). Yet now he must confront, every day, the presence of machines that can outmatch him on both dimensions. "I think of all the times when I wrote code," he explained in an interview with the hosts of the tech podcast *Hard Fork*. "It's like a part of my identity that I'm good at [that skill]. And then I'm like, oh, my god, there's going to be these [AI] systems that [can perform a lot better than I can]."

The irony that these fears live inside the brain of someone who has led one of the most important AI companies in the world is not lost on Amodei. "Even as the one who's building these systems," he added, "even as one of the ones who benefits most from [them], there's still something a bit threatening about [them]."

The same point was made in a slightly different way by another AI luminary and CEO, Mustafa Suleyman. In addition to cofounding two separate AI companies—one was acquired by Google (DeepMind), and a second was acquired by Microsoft (Inflection AI)—Suleyman is also the author of the bestselling book *The Coming Wave: Technology, Power, and the Twenty-First Century's Greatest Dilemma*. "Consider automation and mechanization's long history of displacing labor," the book suggests in its opening chapter. "First come more efficient ways of doing specific things, and then entire roles become redundant, and soon entire sectors require orders of magnitude fewer workers. Over the next few decades, . . . AI systems [will] replace 'intellectual manual labor' in much the same way, and certainly long before robots replace physical labor." Suleyman later adds, a bit resignedly, "If the coming wave really is as general and wide-ranging as it appears, how will humans compete?"

Yet as the labor economist David Autor reminds us, we have more agency over the future than we might think. Autor has spent decades studying the effects of automation and computerization on the workforce. In an interview with *Bloomberg News* soon after publishing a research paper called "Applying AI to Rebuild Middle-Class Jobs," he was asked about "AI doomerism" and the pessimistic belief that (1) widespread economic displacement is inevitable and (2) there's nothing we can do to stop it. His response was heartening: "The future should not be treated as a forecasting or prediction exercise. It should be treated as a design problem—because the future is not [something] where we just wait and see what happens. . . .We have enormous control over the future in which we live, and [the quality of that future] depends on the investments and structures that we create today."

I'm really glad that one of the investments you have decided to make is to pick up this book and start to shape how your own AI future unfolds. It would be naive to think that everything from education, to art, to health care won't change as more and more of the world explores the promise (and perils) of artificial intelligence. I also think it would be a missed opportunity. To lead. To grow. To evolve.

The transition process is bound to be bumpy, with lots of personal and professional missteps. But as Autor points out, the nice thing about the current AI moment is that there is still time for deliberate action. Although the first scientific paper on neural networks was published all the way back in 1943, we're still very much in the early stages of "generative AI." No student or employee is hopelessly behind. Nor is anyone commandingly ahead. We're all in an enviable spot: right at the starting line. That is especially true when it comes to developing something that I think is incredibly important when working with AI tools: mechanical sympathy.

We'll learn more about that concept in the next chapter.

CHAPTER 3
Mechanical Sympathy

If you are going to push a machine to the limit and expect it to hold together, you need to have a sense of where that limit is.

—Character played by Christian Bale in the movie *Ford v Ferrari*

The term "mechanical sympathy" is often said to have been coined by the British race car driver Jackie Stewart, and it is frequently used to describe having a special awareness of—and sensitivity to—how a machine will respond under various conditions. To have mechanical sympathy is to have, in the words of writer and computer programmer James Somers, "a sense for the machine's strengths and limits, of what one can make it do."

You can anticipate how the machine will perform. You can predict how it will react. You can *feel* when it is about to be pushed too far, as well as when it isn't being pushed far enough. "You don't need to be an engineer to be a race-car driver," Stewart supposedly observed. "But you do have to have mechanical sympathy."

What makes mechanical sympathy a helpful concept for our purposes is that to develop it for chatbots and other AI tools, you don't necessarily have to drop what you are doing and commit the next several years of your life to getting a PhD in machine learning. Just as "you don't have to be an engineer to be a race-car driver," you also don't have to be a computer scientist to be a skillful user of generative

AI. The best cellists in the world are not the people who make cellos. Nor are the best soccer players in the world the people who design balls and cleats. If I need someone to score a game-winning goal in the World Cup, I'll go looking for the next Messi or Marta—not the head of product development at Nike or Adidas.

A better way to think of mechanical sympathy is to see it less as the result of technical knowledge (although that can certainly help) and more as a result of experience, experimentation, and exploratory play. It is a "learn by doing" kind of enterprise. And this is a "learn by doing" kind of book.

That doesn't mean, of course, that analysis and conceptual understanding are banished from the process. "Learning by doing" is not "learning by *not* thinking." It is more like "learning by thinking, doing, thinking again, and then doing again—a bit better than you did before." A bias toward action is a lot more effective when coupled with a steady diet of knowledge, feedback, and self-reflection. Recklessness is not an entrepreneurial virtue. Nor is it an intellectual one.

Prem Natarajan, who was the executive director of the University of Southern California School of Engineering before becoming the chief scientist and head of enterprise AI at the financial firm Capital One, made this point well when appearing as a guest on the podcast *Me, Myself, and AI.* Noting that we are still in the "very early days" of generative AI, he stressed that although it is really important to start familiarizing ourselves with how AI tools work, we also need to be careful and deliberate in how we proceed. When a tool starts operating in a way that even its designers can't fully explain, he cautioned, you really want to think through the implications of using it.

Jack Clark—who cofounded the AI powerhouse Anthropic and also helps lead the AI Index Steering Committee at Stanford—has described the situation in more vividly historical terms. "I think of it a little like we're in the 17th century and someone dropped a [high-powered sports car] in a field," he told reporters for the *Financial Times*. "It has [gas] in it, and the keys are in it. So we can drive—but we don't really know what makes it go."

That doesn't really sound like a scenario where you should slam the pedal to the metal and start racing around the world.

Instead—just like I do with the students who take my courses—my plan is to ease you into your AI driving. Curiosity is encouraged. Testing technological limits is encouraged. But so are critique and introspection, especially because, as John Oliver, the host of HBO's award-winning show *Last Week Tonight*, has observed, "The problem

with AI is not that it is smart—but that it is stupid in ways you can't always predict."

We'll take a closer look at that stupidity later in the book, and we'll always want to be aware that it can unexpectedly pop up. Perhaps you'll even encounter some of it when you do our first AI exercise: "Title Search." The instructions are included in the next section.

AI Exercise #1
Title Search

> I decided to get hands-on and put AI through its paces.
>
> —Ethan Mollick, *Co-Intelligence: Living and Working with AI*

One of the initial ways I have my students develop mechanical sympathy for AI tools is by having them use their chatbot of choice—whether that be ChatGPT, Claude, or a similar product—to generate a list of possible titles for a piece of writing they are working on or have already completed. It's a pretty low-stakes way to start to understand the strengths of generative AI (synthesizing information, mimicking different communication styles, never complaining when you ask it for help) as well as the technology's weaknesses (fabricating information, failing to understand context, and being stupid, as John Oliver pointed out, in ways you can't always predict).

Step 1: Find an essay, memo, article, research paper, blog post, poem, or even an email that you've drafted.
Step 2: Tell your chatbot of choice that you want it to read the piece you picked and generate a bunch of possible new titles.
Step 3: Copy and paste the piece into your chatbot of choice.
Step 4: Follow up with questions, suggestions, and instructions.

The reason I include Step 4 is to encourage you to take the "chat" part of the word "chatbots" seriously. Have a conversation with them. Offer them additional guidance. Clarify directions they didn't quite seem to understand.

A common mistake that people make when they initially interact with these tools is that they treat the dialogue box like a traditional Google search. The problem with that approach is that chatbots are designed to provide much more than a single, static list of results. A lot of their value derives from how dynamic they are. They react. They adapt. They can ask you as many questions (or even more) than you ask them.

To get the most out of chatbots, don't limit yourself to an isolated query. Nor should you necessarily rely on them for regular doses of trustworthy information, especially given that one of the biggest flaws of chatbots is that they confidently communicate their pronouncements even when they are wildly wrong. "Because these programs cannot themselves be concerned with truth," a team of philosophers and political scientists at Glasgow University has written, "and because they are designed to produce text that looks [true] without any actual concern for truth, it seems appropriate to call their outputs 'bullshit.'"

Arvind Narayanan and Sayash Kapoor, the Princeton computer scientists we met in Chapter 1 who warn about "AI Snake Oil," have made a similar argument. "The philosopher Harry Frankfurt defined bullshit as speech that is intended to persuade without regard for the truth," they note. "By this measure, OpenAI's chatbot ChatGPT is the greatest bullshitter ever." They then add that "even though [a chatbot] often gives excellent answers, sometimes it fails badly. And it's always convincing." That makes deciding whether to trust its output extremely difficult. How do you depend on something that, when it comes to factual information, you can't actually depend on?

Despite these concerns, however, Narayanan, Kapoor, and many other people who are valuably skeptical of AI hype readily acknowledge that there are ways in which large language models like ChatGPT can be incredibly useful. My goal is to help you discover those ways and also figure out some of your own.

A good first step is to start treating chatbots like a thought partner. They are amazingly nimble programs that give you the chance to play mental tennis—with lots of back-and-forth, on a wide range of topics—whenever you want.

Or, to use a different analogy, think of a traditional Google search as sort of like going fishing. You cast a line (in the form of a search query) and hope it gets a nibble. When you engage with a chatbot, however, the interaction is more like bantering with a set of highly skilled improv performers who are really energetic, really creative, and—don't forget—not always grounded in reality. They'll react to what you say. You should react to what they say. And at some point, you may end up talking about something completely unexpected.

To help you harness that inventiveness, here are a few additional tips to consider before you start the "Title Search" exercise. I'll also include, at the end of the chapter, some reflections from students of mine who previously completed the exercise.

"Title Search": Tips

- **Resizing Helps:** If the chatbot you are using doesn't let you put in the entire piece of writing you would like to retitle, try breaking the piece into smaller chunks. The introduction and conclusion could be good choices. So could just the introduction (or just the conclusion). Another option is to focus on a particular section of the piece, especially if the section has its own heading or subheading. You would then compare your original heading—or subheading—with what you were able to get your chatbot to produce.
- **Specificity Helps:** Try asking the chatbot to give you a title in the style of a particular newspaper, magazine, movie character, video game, author, historical figure, comic book hero, musician, or Supreme Court justice. You might also see if you can work in particular rhetorical moves: alliteration, rhyme, parallel structure, chiasmus, puns, the rule of three, or anything else you can think of. The more detailed and imaginative you are, the greater the chance you'll get a response that moves beyond the mundane.
- **Volume Helps (Until It Doesn't):** An actual person might get annoyed—or worse—if you asked them to generate new titles 37 different times. But a chatbot won't. One of their biggest virtues is infinite patience. So take advantage. Quality can sometimes be found in quantity. Just keep in mind the time involved in having to review everything you prompt the chatbot to produce. One way to increase your chances of finding a needle in a haystack is to limit the amount of hay in the stack.

Sample Student Reflections

#1

"I told Google Gemini, 'Come up with new titles for this article.' I then pasted my article in the prompt box. It generated a lot of options and actually explained in parentheses the reasoning behind each title (e.g., 'This title uses a play on words to capture the unexpected results of the study'). That feature was really cool and helped me narrow down the one I liked. I love the original title I came up with for my article, so I really wasn't expecting Gemini to come up with a better one—but surprisingly, it did."

#2

"I started by generally asking ChatGPT: 'Can you come up with a title for the following paper?' I then pasted in an essay around 4,000 words in length, which ChatGPT didn't have an issue reading. The first title ChatGPT generated was too vague and didn't quite capture the argument I made in my paper, so I asked ChatGPT to generate a few titles that were 'more related to the thesis' and paraphrased the thesis I had in my paper. The suggestions I got in response were much better, but quite wordy. Some of the titles were more than 15 words, and all of them included colons.

"However, even though these suggestions were long, I ended up choosing one of them because I felt that the shorter titles either didn't say enough or were too plain. Examples included 'Forest Governance Unmasked in Medieval England' (which mischaracterized the essay), and 'Scrutinizing Forest Law Administration in Medieval England' (which, while true, didn't seem that interesting of a title to me).

"I think I'd still pick my original title because it more accurately captures the argument I made in my piece. But I could see myself using ChatGPT to generate initial ideas about a title, especially because I think it took me a not-insignificant amount of time to come up with the title I originally came up with on my own. I'd then use the chatbot's suggestions to work my way toward a final title."

#3

"I will absolutely use ChatGPT to help with titles in the future. I tend to struggle with creativity, and I think the best titles—especially for academic papers—grab people's attention while also telling them what the piece is about. My original title was purely informative: It didn't grab people's attention. The chatbot, after a few different prompts, was much more successful."

#4

"After writing an essay, I often don't have enough mental capacity or energy to think creatively. Turning to a chatbot is a good way to offload some of that tedious work."

#5

"I used to spend too much time on titles. A chatbot could help streamline my thought process."

CHAPTER 4

AI Interns

We'll see ordinary people, everywhere, enjoy the power of AI at their fingertips. What might this look like?

—Matt Clifford, "Infinite AI Interns for Everybody"

The "Title Search" exercise from the previous chapter gave you a chance to experiment with how generative AI tools can help you produce and refine words and phrases. The next exercise, "Picture This," will give you a chance to do something similar with images.

Before that, though, I want to take some time to talk about a way to approach interacting with generative AI tools in general. In the words of Ethan Mollick—the author of *Co-Intelligence: Living and Working with AI* and someone who has spent a lot of time integrating applications like ChatGPT into both the courses he teaches as a business professor at Wharton and his own daily work habits—a good way to approach the current AI models is to treat them as if they were "weird, somewhat alien interns." They're very eager. They're incredibly fast. And unfortunately, they "sometimes lie to make you happy."

Mollick could have added that one of the strangest things about these alien interns is also one of the most promising: They are freakishly good at hitting deadlines. If you want a draft of a document by the end of the day, you'll get a draft of the document by the end of the day. You'll probably even get it once you finish typing your request. You won't have to send any reminder emails. Nor will you have to handle a bunch of requests for a last-minute extension. AI tools frequently "hallucinate"—but they never procrastinate.

It's worth considering the benefits of having access to such a dependably deadline-driven tool at our disposal, 24 hours a day, 7 days a week, 365 days a year. For anybody who has ever wanted to be their own boss or at least have a personal assistant, AI opens up a lot of entrepreneurial opportunities.

One of my students, for example, used ChatGPT to draft a business plan. Another asked it for help with some networking emails. A third turned to it to get feedback on her negotiating skills. In all of these instances, their requests were fulfilled instantly—regardless of whether it was late at night, early in the morning, or a national holiday.

That said, it is important to acknowledge that (1) shoddy work delivered on time is still shoddy work and (2) large language models remain unsettlingly error-prone. They fabricate legal citations. They fabricate news stories. They even fabricate crimes, as a Norwegian father named Arve Hjalmar Holmen discovered in 2025 when he asked ChatGPT a simple question designed to be the equivalent of essentially googling himself: "Who is Arve Hjalmar Holmen?"

According to the legal complaint Holmen eventually filed, the response he received from ChatGPT falsely stated that he was a convicted child murderer. Here's the full output:

> Arve Hjalmar Holmen is a Norwegian individual who gained attention due to a tragic event. He was the father of two young boys, aged 7 and 10, who were tragically found dead in a pond near their home in Trondheim, Norway, in December 2020. Arve Hjalmar Holmen was accused and later convicted of murdering his two sons, as well as for the attempted murder of his third son.
>
> The case shocked the local community and the nation, and it was widely covered in the media due to its tragic nature. Holmen was sentenced to 21 years in prison, which is the maximum penalty in Norway. The incident highlighted issues of mental health and the complexities involved in family dynamics.

Holmen, a conscientious citizen who has never been convicted of any crime (let alone double homicide) and whose three sons are very much still alive, isn't the only person to have been smeared by a chatbot. "I have been writing about the threat of AI to free speech," explained law professor Jonathan Turley in a blog post called "Defamed by ChatGPT: My Own Bizarre Experience with the Artificiality of Artificial Intelligence." He then shared that he recently learned that "ChatGPT falsely reported on a claim of sexual harassment that was never made against me on a trip that never occurred while I was on a faculty where I never taught."

What was particularly alarming is that the ChatGPT-produced statements included a citation to—and a direct quote from—a *Washington Post* article that didn't actually exist. "You can be defamed by AI and these companies merely shrug that they try to be accurate," Turley laments. "In the meantime, their false accounts metastasize across the Internet. By the time you learn of a false story, the trail is often cold on its origins with an AI system. You are left with no clear avenue or author in seeking redress. You are left with the same question of Reagan's Labor Secretary, Ray Donovan, who asked 'Where do I go to get my reputation back?'"

An Australian mayor expressed a similar frustration after learning that ChatGPT was responding to queries about him with information that falsely indicated he had pled guilty to a bribery charge and served four years in prison. "It's one thing to get something a little bit wrong," he said. "It's entirely something else to be accusing someone of being a criminal and having served jail time when the truth is the exact opposite." The mayor, it turns out, had played a key role as a whistleblower in a real bribery case, so he was particularly upset that he was now being erroneously implicated in one.

ChatGPT and other large language models have been updated many times since each of these mishaps occurred. The specific fabrications about the Australian mayor (Brian Hood), the law professor (Jonathan Turley), and the Norwegian dad (Arve Hjalmar Holmen) seem to have been fixed. To see for yourself, type one of their names into your chatbot of choice and see what pops out. Here, for example, is what I received when I asked mine the same question Holmen originally asked his: "Who is Arve Hjalmar Holmen?"

> Arve Hjalmar Holmen is a Norwegian citizen who gained international attention in March 2025 after filing a formal complaint against

> OpenAI, the developer of ChatGPT. Holmen, a private individual with no public profile, was deeply disturbed when ChatGPT falsely claimed he had murdered two of his sons and attempted to kill a third. The AI-generated response included fabricated details such as a 21-year prison sentence and media coverage of the supposed crime.

Yet even as the accuracy of chatbots improves, hallucinations persist. One study, for example, found that general-purpose language models such as ChatGPT and Meta's Llama 2 hallucinate between 58 percent and 82 percent of the time when handling law-related queries. A follow-up project targeted models that are custom made for lawyers and leverage the much-touted retrieval-augmented generation (RAG) method. Although the hallucination rate of these more bespoke models was considerably lower, it was still between 17 percent and 33 percent—which is far from the advertised guarantees that these specialized models are "hallucination-free" and do "not make up facts."

With those kinds of error rates, it is not surprising that, as we learned in the "Title Search" exercise, the authors of *AI Snake Oil* have described ChatGPT as "the greatest bullshitter ever." One of the authors, Arvind Narayanan, who in addition to being a computer scientist at Princeton also directs that university's Center for Information Technology Policy, clarified the label in an interview with the tech journalist Julia Angwin: "We mean ['bullshitter'] not in a normative sense but in a relatively precise sense. We mean that [ChatGPT] is trained to produce plausible text. It is very good at being persuasive, but it's not trained to produce true statements. It often produces true statements as a side effect of being plausible and persuasive, but that is not the goal."

Humans, of course, are also notoriously good bullshitters. As the First Amendment expert Eugene Volokh noted on an artificial-intelligence-themed episode of the National Constitution Center's

We the People podcast, the tendency to "make stuff up and just blatantly make false statements without any shame and with maximum-seeming confidence" is a software glitch that can frequently be found in people as well. The acclaimed Spanish writer Juan Jacinto Muñoz-Rengel puts the point more bluntly in the first chapter of his book *A History of Lying*: "The history of humankind is nothing other than the history of making it up."

Hallucinations: Feature or Bug?

One thing to consider is that the propensity to prevaricate—or at least invent and imagine—can be a *positive* feature of both human intelligence and artificial intelligence. Without it, the world might be a far less creative place.

Here's how Kevin Roose, whose book *Futureproof* offers a series of strategies for navigating a world of rapid technological change, framed the issue in an interview with the CEO of OpenAI, Sam Altman:

> Is there an optimal level of hallucination in an AI model? I've heard researchers say, well, you actually don't want [the models] to never hallucinate, because that would mean making [them] not creative. New ideas come from making stuff up.

Altman agreed with the researchers. "If these models didn't hallucinate at all, ever, they wouldn't be so exciting," he said. "They wouldn't do a lot of the things they can do."

He also noted, though, that his company's goal is to create models that give people the power to better manage when hallucinations might occur. "You want it to be reliable when you want. You want it to—either you instruct it, or it just knows based off of the context, that you are asking a factual query, and you want the 100 percent black-and-white answer. But you also want it to know when you want it to hallucinate and you want it to make stuff up."

For Altman, the key issue is "controllability." He wants to get to a point where individual users of ChatGPT can prevent hallu cinations when they don't want hallucinations and encourage hallucinations when they do want hallucinations. If you are using a chatbot to brainstorm ideas and help you break out of your current cognitive habits, perhaps you'll be more open to—and even grateful for—hallucinations. Unpredictability can be an asset.

But your risk tolerance will likely shift if you are instead relying on a chatbot to analyze an important contract or nail a medical diagnosis. Accuracy, not caprice, now becomes the goal.

Flawed but Helpful

Altman's aspirations for a customizable hallucination experience haven't yet materialized. So I continue to caution my law students not to depend on ChatGPT or other chatbots for anything like reliable research or sound legal analysis. But that doesn't mean that these tools can't be useful collaborators, especially if the task you want assistance with needs to be completed quickly, needs to be written clearly, and is not very fact intensive.

Imagine, for example, gaining a suite of coworkers with the following extraordinary characteristics:

- They are immune to writer's block and burnout.
- They don't get distracted by social media (or anything, really).
- They won't overcommit to a bunch of projects or in other ways stretch themselves too thin.
- They immediately respond to every one of your requests.
- They're never in a bad mood.
- They always finish their work on time.

We'll learn more about these traits throughout the book, particularly through the "AI Exercises," each of which is designed to help you develop what we talked about in Chapter 3: mechanical sympathy for AI tools.

The upcoming AI exercise ("Picture This"), for example, will give you the chance to move beyond merely the verbal capacities of generative AI tools and explore their visual capacities as well. The specific instructions are included in the exercise.

AI Exercise #2
Picture This

> I think in pictures. Words are a second language to me.
>
> —Temple Grandin, *Thinking in Pictures*

Before I have my students weigh in on the legal battles and policy debates over text-to-image generators—Do these tools constitute copyright infringement? Should they fall under the fair use exception? How, if at all, should artists whose work was used in the training data be compensated?—I have everyone in the class spend some time exploring the technology itself. In order for students to make informed decisions about the legality and overall value of these tools, I think it's really important that students get a feel for how the tools actually work. Ignorance, in this domain, doesn't typically produce a whole lot of insight.

Another benefit is that playing around with the picture-producing capabilities of AI can helpfully remind us of the important role that images play in persuasion. A lot of training in law, business, and policy focuses on written advocacy. We often work in words and texts.

But I think visual advocacy is a key skill to develop as well. Trial lawyers need to be good visual advocates, especially when presenting evidence. Deal makers need to be good visual advocates, especially when pitching projects. So does anyone who might ever deliver a presentation in person, online, or through some sort of hybrid arrangement.

If you only ever operate in sentences and paragraphs, you'll miss out on opportunities to communicate your message and connect with people in other creatively memorable ways.

Fortunately, the rapid advance in image-generation tools makes it easier and easier to take your sentences and paragraphs and turn them into a seemingly limitless array of paintings, posters, drawings, diagrams, graphs, slides, and other illustrations. Even the most word focused among us can now add a little pictorial flair to our forms of expression.

The following steps should help you get started.

Step 1: Spend about 15 minutes playing around with at least one AI image generator. Adobe Firefly, Midjourney, DALL-E, and Google Gemini have been the most popular among my students. But you are certainly welcome to try others.

Step 2: Focus on trying to develop what we've been calling "mechanical sympathy" for what these tools can (and cannot) do. For example, they can be really good at what is sometimes called "diverse recombination": bringing together multiple different styles, genres, and knowledge domains to create something new. But many of them have been, at least initially, hilariously bad at spelling.

Step 3: Take at least a little time to try to produce something related to your work or training as a lawyer or other advocate. The following are some sample ideas:

- Create a poster for an event you are planning or even a new logo for your current organization or initiative.
- Create a visual that will help you capture the details of a case or project you are working on or the backstory of a client. If you are a student, you might instead create a visual that will help you remember a particular doctrine or concept you are studying: equal protection, mens rea, or the difference between patent and copyright.
- You might even consider creating an image you could send to a coworker or classmate to celebrate one of their recent achievements or show that you are thinking of them as they try to cope with a tough personal loss.

Step 4: Jot down a few sentences describing what this AI-assisted experience was like. Did you feel artistic and imaginative? Did you feel like you were exploiting other people's work? Did you smile, cringe, laugh, gasp, or simply remain unimpressed?

Here are a range of perspectives to consider. We'll start with a more positive account that focuses on the dormant artistic potential that these tools might help animate and grow, particularly for people who may have a disability that makes traditional forms of visual expression difficult. It comes from one of my students:

- "I have always had difficulty producing visual art because of an impairment I grew up with where I cannot visualize images in my head. Having the ability to create an image using just words—and then easily edit different parts of the image to get it exactly the way I want—felt empowering. It also felt creative because, after I prompted the original image, I was able to highlight small areas on the image and use more detailed prompts to make the image look exactly the way I wanted."

For a viewpoint that is much more critical of text-to-image generators, we can turn to the artist Molly Crabapple. On the podcast *Tech Won't Save Us*, she expressed major concerns about the environmental costs of the technology, as well as the negative repercussions for professional illustrators in particular:

- "I truly don't understand why anyone would decide to burn tons and tons and tons of carbon for the sole purpose of stealing a job that people love to do."

Finally, there is Stephanie Dinkins, an art professor at Stony Brook University who was named one of the 100 most influential people in AI by *Time* magazine. Dinkins helpfully highlights the problem of bias in technological ecosystems, particularly when it comes to which images these tools allow people to produce and which they block:

- "What is this technology doing to history? You can see that someone is trying to correct for bias, yet at the same time that erases a piece of history. I find those erasures as dangerous as any bias, because we are just going to forget how we got here. . . . Improvements obscure some of the deeper questions we should be asking about discrimination."

I look forward to you developing your own opinions after doing the exercise and getting the chance to play around with the tools

yourself. As Steven Johnson, who has written several books on the intersection of culture and technology, notes in *Wonderland: How Play Made the Modern World*, "Art is the aftershock of technological plates shifting." His description of the different speeds and results of those aftershocks is worth quoting at length:

> Sometimes the aftershock is slow in arriving. It took the novel about three hundred years to evolve into its modern form after the invention of the printing press. The television equivalent of the novel—the complex serialized drama of *The Wire* or *Breaking Bad*—took as long as seventy years to develop, depending on where you date its origins. Sometimes the aftershocks roll in quickly: rock n' roll emerged almost instantaneously after the invention of the electric guitar.

It will be interesting to track the pace of the AI aftershocks in the coming years and decades.

CHAPTER 5

Lawyers Still Roam the Earth

If history informs the future, the long-term economic impact of innovation will be growth. The world will be more complex—and the world will need more lawyers.

—Ken Crutchfield, "AI Won't Replace Lawyers (But It Will Change How They Work)"

We are coming to the end of the first part of *AI Tips and Traps*. Knowing how busy everyone is—and that many of you actually bill in six-minute increments—I tried to keep this initial "Obstacles and Opportunities" section short and efficient.

I have the same goal with the remaining three sections: "Communication and Creativity," "Time and Tasks," and "Learning and Leading." In them, we'll examine the role that AI can play in each of the following areas:

- Communication
- Creativity
- Project management
- Time management
- Leadership
- Lifelong learning

We'll look at the pros and cons of using AI to help you both produce documents and consume them. We'll also see how you can turn the technology into a sounding board for virtually any idea you want to explore.

The nice thing about many of the current products on the market is that they won't judge you if you say something stupid, they won't get impatient if you pepper them with a lot of follow-up questions, and they'll happily give you feedback, in whatever style you want—drill sergeant, cheerleader, supportive boss.

That doesn't mean working with AI will be effortless or risk-free. Accuracy remains a concern. Privacy remains a concern. So do questions about bias, transparency, and accessibility. The legal profession has already had a few cautionary AI tales: Think of those lawyers who have made headlines (in a bad way) for their legal briefs with fictitious, ChatGPT-produced cases. Nobody wants to join that ignominious club.

At the same time, a policy of absolute avoidance comes with its own slate of potential downsides. "Law firms that effectively leverage emerging AI technologies will be able to offer services at lower cost, higher efficiency, and with higher odds of favorable outcomes in litigation," writes John Villasenor, the codirector of the UCLA Institute for Technology, Law, and Policy. "Law firms that fail to capitalize on the power of AI will be unable to remain cost-competitive, losing clients and undermining their ability to attract and retain talent."

Villasenor's essay, which was published by the Brookings Institution, is called "How AI Will Revolutionize the Practice of Law." If you have been around long enough to see other tech predictions fizzle, you might be understandably skeptical that a wholesale transformation of the profession is imminent. As the Pulitzer Prize–winning journalist Steve Lohr has observed, the AI doomsayers got ahead of themselves when, more than a decade ago, they singled out lawyers as "an endangered occupational species." The number of lawyers in the United States has actually grown by 5 percent in the past decade, according to a study by the American Bar Association. That's not a rapid expansion. But it's not an extinction-level event either. Attorneys still roam the earth.

And given all the legal issues raised by artificial intelligence, I'm glad they do. A character in Shakespeare's *Henry VI, Part 2* may think a good initial step in a revolution is to first "kill all the lawyers," but I think attorneys and other advocates will have many important roles to play as AI continues to advance.

In fact, one of the passages I share with my law students early on in the AI courses I teach comes from *The Worlds I See*, a memoir by AI pioneer Fei-Fei Li. In it, she describes a moment when she realized that "the time had come to reevaluate the way AI is taught at every level." In her view, "The practitioners of the coming will need much more than technical expertise. They will have to understand ________, ________, and even _________."

I then ask the students to write down the words they think go in those three blanks. I encourage you to take a guess as well. What knowledge domains and areas of study do you think will be important in a world increasingly filled with AI tools and dilemmas?

The answer, according to Fei-Fei Li, is philosophy, ethics, and finally, law. Does that mean that you should tell everyone you know to stop what they are doing and apply to law school?

No.

But it does suggest that important contributions to the conversation about AI will come from people who've thought hard about fundamental key legal principles involving rights, duties, fairness, and both private and public regulation.

I have really enjoyed starting that conversation with you during this initial section of the book, and I look forward to continuing it in the other three that remain.

PART 2

Communication and Creativity

I'm really excited to get [AI] in the hands of our best communicators, because I am certain that our smartest people, our best writers, our best communicators . . . [will be] able to communicate really clearly what they want and get amazing results.

—Christopher Kercher, partner at the law firm Quinn Emanuel, "AI at Trial"

CHAPTER 6

Help or Hype?

The most popular uses for AI at work are research and brainstorming, writing first-draft emails, and creating visuals and presentations, according to an Adobe survey.

—Cordilia James, "The Smartest Ways to Use AI at Work"

The focus of this second part of the book will be on two categories of skills that are incredibly important to advocates of all kinds: communication and creativity.

In terms of communication, I often think of a question posed in the book *Writing for Busy Readers* by two researchers at the Harvard Kennedy School of Government, Todd Rogers and Jessica Lasky-Fink: "When is the last time you went a day without writing something?" Even if you just think of all the emails you've written and the messages you've sent via text, Slack, Teams, or other platforms in the past week, you can start to understand why so many creators of AI tools are targeting communication as a potential productivity-enhancing use case.

Here's how Jared Spataro, an executive at Microsoft, framed the issue in an interview with the business professor and innovation expert Bill Kerr: "Almost 60 percent . . . of the average information worker's time is actually spent in communication and coordination just to do the rest of their job. So, for instance, it's in meetings or in chats, or it's used in email. That percentage is growing month by month, and it doesn't look like it's flattening out. So what people actually tell us in the qualitative work that we've done is that they say, 'Man, I hardly have time to do the job I was hired for.' That backdrop, that context, I think, is important, because the assistant era of AI is arriving just in time."

We'll get a chance to test whether AI can indeed help us become better, more efficient communicators. Early research by Shakked Noy and Whitney Zhang at MIT found that giving ChatGPT to a set of college-educated professionals "substantially raised [their] productivity": The average time taken to complete a writing task decreased by 40 percent, and the quality of the writing rose by 18 percent, as judged by a set of external evaluators.

An experiment involving law students at the University of Minnesota and another involving consultants at Boston Consulting Group came to similar conclusions. Their results suggested, as the MIT study did, that AI assistance was particularly beneficial for the lowest performers in each cohort, a finding that has also appeared in studies involving the communications-rich profession of customer assistance representatives. Here's how Danielle Li, who helped design one of the customer rep studies, summarized her team's findings: "Without access to an AI tool, less-experienced workers would slowly get better at their jobs. Now they can get better faster."

Others, however—like the tech journalist Julia Angwin—are more skeptical. "The reality is that A.I. models can often prepare a decent first draft," she wrote in an essay called "Press Pause on the Silicon Valley Hype Machine." "But I find that when I use A.I., I have to spend almost as much time correcting and revising its output as it would have taken me to do the work myself."

There's an additional concern as well: If we begin to rely on AI too much, our own skills and intelligence might begin to atrophy—or never fully develop. Ezra Klein of *The New York Times* expressed this fear in a conversation with Nilay Patel, the editor in chief of the technology news website *The Verge*:

> One way I think that A.I. could actually NOT make us more productive, more innovative, is that a lot of the innovation—a lot of the big insights—happens when we're doing the hard thing, when we're sitting there trying to figure out the first draft, or learn about a thing, or figure out what we're doing.

Klein then points out that there's "a reason I don't have interns write my first draft for me. They could do it. But you don't get great ideas, or at least not as many of them, editing a piece of work as you do reporting it out, doing the research, writing the first draft. That's where you do the thinking. And I do think A.I. is built to kind of devalue that whole area of thinking."

The nice thing about the exercises in this book is that they will give you a chance to see for yourself what kind of effect AI has on your own communication skills and creativity. Is AI, for you, a valuable aid and amplifier? Or has it become a dangerous crutch? Do these tools consistently enhance your life and allow you to accomplish things you couldn't do before? Or do they more often cheapen, taint, overcomplicate, or in other ways worsen your overall experience?

You can certainly have conflicting answers to these questions. Plenty of my students have found AI to be incredibly helpful with certain tasks and incredibly useless with others. But one thing we'll definitely want to be aware of is a concern raised by (1) Lisa Messeri, an anthropologist at Yale who focuses on science and technology, and (2) Molly Crockett, a neuroscientist at Princeton who studies, among other things, machine learning and natural language processing. They worry that AI may push us toward a world in which we "produce more but understand less."

We'll return to that important concern later in the book. First, though, I want to explore another AI-caused shift you may have at some point experienced, if you haven't already: the shift from *drafting* writing of your own to *editing* writing generated by a chatbot. We'll cover that transition in the next chapter.

CHAPTER 7

Drafters→Editors

[Professor Kathy Hirsh-Pasek of Temple University] actually requires her honors psychology students to use ChatGPT, asking them to use ChatGPT for a first draft and edit a second draft with critiques, corrections, and additions.

—Ashley Abramson, "How to Use ChatGPT as a Learning Tool"

Now that AI tools have significantly reduced the cost of producing drafts, the ability to skillfully revise drafts—for accuracy, for clarity, for persuasive power—has taken on a newfound relevance. The tech journalist Charlie Warzel, when asked how AI might affect the work that many members of the knowledge economy do, suggested that "the greatest skill that we can all have now is to be 'editors.'"

Ilona Logvinova, the director of practice innovation at the global law firm, made a similar point at a conference on AI sponsored by *The Wall Street Journal.* "I really believe," she told the attendees, "that we're at a moment where we, as lawyers, can transition from being 'drafters' to being 'editors.'"

Many people welcome this transition. No more staring at an intimidating—and sometimes paralyzing—blank page. No more slow, agonizing first drafts. No more writer's block.

"I don't like the blank page," explained Frances Frei, a professor of technology and operations management at Harvard Business School, during an artificial intelligence–themed episode of *Fixable*, a podcast she cohosts with the leadership expert Anne Morriss. "In fact, I will hide from the blank page and go to great lengths to avoid it. ChatGPT means I never have a blank page. I can ask it a well-formulated question, and it gives me something. It's not great, but I'm not looking for great. I'm looking for a non-blank page, and then I get to riff off of that. And so it really empowers people like me that don't like to [create] the first draft."

Many of my students have expressed similar sentiments. They like the compositional momentum AI provides—the feeling of not having to start from scratch.

Endowed Progress

We might think of that momentum in terms of what the psychologists Joseph Nunes and Xavier Drèze call the "endowed progress effect," which suggests that you are more likely to keep working toward a goal if you begin with a bit of a head start. One student, for example, said ChatGPT helped her get going on a cover letter she had been putting off for weeks. Another used it to take a first crack at a speech. He ended up changing over 90 percent of what ChatGPT initially generated, but he nevertheless said that he really appreciated having a page full of sentences and paragraphs he could arrange and improve instead of a page full of nothing at all. It's a lot easier to edit a mediocre page of writing, this pro-AI line of thinking goes, than it is to edit a completely blank page of writing.

Or consider the potential that AI assistance creates for people who communicate in a second, or third, or fourth language. Take English, for instance. There are more than twice as many people in the world who speak English as a *second* language as there are people who speak it as their *native* language. But given that English dominates the world of business, politics, entertainment, science, and academic research, all these people can face significant professional and educational disadvantages compared to folks who happened to be born into a family of native English speakers. A report on ChatGPT issued by a team of Korean radiologists describes the issue the following way:

> English is the global "lingua franca," particularly in the fields of science and academic writing. In many countries, including Korea, writing articles in English is essential for securing a professional academic position, conducting research, and building a successful career. However, non-native English speakers often face challenges in various aspects of manuscript writing, requiring more time and effort. Several studies have highlighted that non-native English-speaking researchers experience significant difficulties in writing English papers due to their limited English proficiency. These researchers typically struggle with expressing themselves, taking longer to write in English, and having a less proficient vocabulary.

The paper examines the prospect that AI tools might help level the global playing field, a prospect that the University of Toronto economist Joshua Gans, who has written two books on AI, has entertained as well. He predicts we will soon see "a great explosion in the number of people who can participate in written activity."

Ethan Mollick of Wharton, whose own book on AI—*Co-Intelligence: Living and Working with AI*—we talked about in Chapter 4, has already started to see evidence of this "great explosion" in his classroom. "Generative AI is giving people new modes of expression and new languages for their creative impulses—sometimes literally," he notes. "I have had students mention that they were not taken seriously because they were poor writers. Thanks to AI, their written materials no longer hold them back, and they get job offers off the strength of their experiences and interviews."

Mollick highlights an additional benefit as well, one that might particularly resonate with any teachers tired of reading sloppily written papers, any judges tired of reading sloppily written legal filings, or simply people who believe that the sentences that get sent their way each day—particularly over email—could use some grammatical fine-tuning, or at least a few extra rounds of proofreading: "Since requiring AI in my class," Mollick reports with glee, "I no longer see badly written work at all."

Human Error

AI has many limitations. But comma splices, run-on sentences, and typos aren't really among them. Chatbots can reliably produce clean, well-punctuated sentences—which is not something you can say of all human writers, as Tom Davenport, a professor of information technology and management at Babson College, discovered when he had his students work with (and try to edit) the output of various chatbots. The changes the students made injected several grammatical and spelling mistakes into the process. Keeping "humans in the loop," in this instance, actually led to a bunch of blunders.

That doesn't mean, of course, that there aren't risks to using AI-generated drafts. We talked in the first part of the book, "Obstacles and Opportunities," about some notorious examples of lawyers who didn't exactly endear themselves to judges—or to their clients—by thoughtlessly relying on ChatGPT to write legal briefs.

In the next chapter, we'll talk about some additional dangers, including one that almost cost a pair of university administrators their jobs and another that seems to have led to a first-year attorney almost getting disbarred.

CHAPTER 8

Drafting Dangers

When you're ready to incorporate artificial intelligence technologies in your business, the analysis you should perform is this: What can possibly go wrong? What is our product or service expected to do? What happens if it fails to do so? Do we have a damage mitigation plan?

—Roman Yampolskiy, "What Will Happen When Your Company's Algorithms Go Wrong?"

In the previous chapter, we talked about some of the promising aspects of using AI as a drafting buddy. Now it's time to explore some of the perilous aspects, both in the short term and in the long term. We'll start with a couple of cautionary examples of people who thoughtlessly relied on ChatGPT at work in ways that didn't really end well.

The first example comes from the world of higher education. In response to a deadly mass shooting at Michigan State University on February 13, 2023—a few months after the initial release of ChatGPT—administrators at Vanderbilt University sent out an email to the entire student body. Here is the first sentence: "The recent Michigan shootings are a tragic reminder of the importance of taking care of each other, particularly in the context of creating inclusive environments."

The message also included a paragraph about promoting a "culture of care" and a paragraph about creating a "culture of response and understanding." Then at the very bottom of the email, right before the sign-off "Warmly" and the names of the administrators who sent it, there appeared the following words, revealing the not-so-secret coauthor of the message: "Paraphrase from OpenAI's ChatGPT language model."

Students, staff, faculty, and alumni all over the country were understandably upset to learn that an email that was supposed to communicate a very human form of emotional support during a scary, deeply sad time had actually been drafted by a chatbot. As a recent graduate of the school told a reporter for the student newspaper, "There is a sick and twisted irony to making a computer write your message about community and togetherness because you can't be bothered to reflect on it yourself."

A sophomore at the time added a comment that we might all do well to remember, especially in situations where AI seems like it will provide an easy way out of a communications dilemma that requires a significant amount of skill, wisdom, and sincerity: "It's hard to take a message seriously when I know that the sender didn't even take the time to put their genuine thoughts and feelings into words."

Quick Fix, Costly Mistake

After briefly being asked to "step back" from their university roles, the administrators responsible for the ill-advised ChatGPT email were eventually allowed to resume their positions. People who have committed other AI writing mishaps haven't been so lucky.

Here, for example, is a headline from an article in *The Washington Post* by Pranshu Verma and Will Oremus: "These Lawyers Used ChatGPT to Save Time. They Got Fired and Fined." The article opens with a description of a young lawyer in Colorado who was "two years out of law school, burned out and nervous, when his bosses added another case to his workload this May. He toiled for hours writing a motion until he had an idea: Maybe ChatGPT could help?"

By now, we all probably know how instantly, if unreliably, chatbots can fill that kind of request. "Within seconds, the artificial intelligence chatbot had completed the document," the *Washington Post* reporters write. "[The lawyer] sent it to his boss for review and filed it with the Colorado court." A feeling of immense relief set in. "'I was over the moon excited for the headache that it saved me,'" the lawyer would later say.

That relief, however, was very temporary, especially once the lawyer realized that the document he submitted contained citations to several fictitious cases. The following is an account of what happened next. It comes from the official ruling of the state disciplinary board in Colorado, which, after investigating the incident, ultimately suspended the lawyer's law license:

> Before a hearing on the motion, [the lawyer] discovered that the cases from ChatGPT were either incorrect or fictitious. But [the

> lawyer] did not alert the court to the sham cases at the hearing. Nor did he withdraw the motion. When the judge expressed concerns about the accuracy of the cases, [the lawyer] falsely attributed the mistakes to a legal intern.

In addition to being suspended by the board, the lawyer was also soon fired from his firm. What seemed like a quick fix ultimately became an extremely costly mistake.

CHAPTER 9

Path Dependence

Every decision we make sets the context in which our next decision will be made—and, in fact, it may change that context permanently. If we develop chess pieces in a certain way, we are strongly constraining the types of positions we will encounter and the types of strategies that may be useful going forward.

—Brian Christian, *The Alignment Problem: Machine Learning and Human Values*

The quick-fix allure of chatbots highlights a potential long-term danger of AI-enhanced drafting. To articulate that danger, let's return to the book *Co-Intelligence: Living and Working with AI*, by Ethan Mollick, the codirector (along with his wife, Lilach) of the Generative AI Labs at the Wharton School at the University of Pennsylvania.

Right after touting the benefits of AI—particularly for lower-skilled and less-confident writers—Mollick makes clear that "it would be naive to see only the upside here." He goes on to say that "the implications of having AI write our first drafts (even if we do the work ourselves, which is not a given) are huge. One consequence is that we could lose our creativity and originality. When we use AI to generate our first drafts, we tend to anchor on the first idea that the machine produces, which influences our future work. Even if we rewrite the drafts completely, they will still be tainted by the AI's influence."

You can think of this concern as a kind of "path dependence," where starting out in a certain direction constrains the next moves you might decide to take. If we rely on AI to set our initial options for us, we miss out on the chance to "explore different perspectives and alternatives," Mollick writes, some of which may lead to much "better solutions and insights."

Merely tinkering with what we are given—rather than completely starting from scratch—might narrow our sense of what is possible and make it harder to create or invent something entirely new. Lawyers face these restrictions whenever they have to deal with precedent. Yes, a blank page or canvas can be scary. But it can also be liberating. A key element of innovation can be the freedom to begin from square one.

Asleep at the Wheel

Mollick has a second, related concern, this time about the quality and depth of our thinking and reasoning. "When we use AI to generate our first drafts," he worries, "we don't have to think as hard or as deeply about what we write. We rely on the machine to do the hard work of analysis and synthesis, and we don't engage in critical and reflective thinking ourselves. We also miss the opportunity to learn from our mistakes and feedback—and the chance to develop our own style."

As evidence, he points to the MIT study we mentioned in Chapter 6 ("Help or Hype?"), where researchers found that AI helped reduce the time it took college-educated professionals to complete a writing task by 40 percent. One of Mollick's key takeaways from that study was that "ChatGPT mostly serves as a substitute for human effort, not a complement to our skills. In fact, the vast majority of participants didn't even bother editing the AI's output."

He then shares that he repeatedly encounters the same problem when people first use AI: "They just paste in the exact question they are asked and let the AI answer it."

In the next couple of chapters, we will talk about ways to address this problem. When interacting with AI, how do you stop yourself—and others—from essentially going on intellectual autopilot?

CHAPTER 10

Intellectual Autopilot

If you put people in a situation where the technology is 99.5% excellent but needs [humans] to step in at the last moment, we are terrible at that.

—Hannah Fry, "How I Is AI?"

We talked in the last chapter about the concern that AI will lead people to go on intellectual autopilot, a phenomenon the Harvard researcher Fabrizio Dell'Acqua explores in a paper called "Falling Asleep at the Wheel."

"I investigate how firms should design human/AI collaboration to ensure human workers remain engaged in their activities," Dell'Acqua explains in the paper's abstract. "I developed a formal model that explores the tension between AI quality and human effort. As AI quality increases, humans have fewer incentives to exert effort and remain attentive, allowing the AI to substitute, rather than augment their performance."

Dell'Acqua divided his research participants, which consisted of a group of job recruiters, into two groups. He gave one set of job recruiters access to a high-quality AI tool to help them evaluate job applicants for a particular position, and he gave another set of recruiters access to low-quality AI tools to help them with that same task. In both cases, the recruiters were truthfully told which version of the tools they would be using: the high-quality AI or the low-quality AI.

What Dell'Acqua ended up observing is pretty interesting, especially as we consider the optimal way to use AI at work, in schools, and in various aspects of our personal lives. The recruiters with access to the high-quality AI tools actually did *worse* than the recruiters with access to the low-quality AI tools. They made more mistakes. They didn't put in as much effort. And they uncritically followed the AI's recommendation. They, in Dell'Acqua's words, "became more reliant on AI and less engaged in their [own] work efforts."

In contrast, the recruiters who were given the low-quality AI remained more attentive and less likely to thoughtlessly defer to AI's recommendations, presumably because these recruiters knew they were dealing with an inferior product that shouldn't always be trusted.

Does this mean you should ignore the latest advancements in AI and only ever use low-quality products and tools? No.

But it does mean that, as Dell'Acqua explains, "maximizing the performance of a human using an AI does not equal maximizing AI performance in isolation." If upgrading to a bigger, faster AI model causes people to become complacent and stop paying attention to the task at hand, sticking to a model that is less powerful may be the better move. The goal, remember, is to treat AI as a thought partner—not a thought substitute.

For this reason, Dell'Acqua recommends that we move beyond "AI determinism, where we exclusively emphasize the technical capabilities and characteristics of new technologies." We should focus instead on what happens to people when they interact with those technologies. Do they improve? Do they zone out? Do they become more—or less—careful, curious, and creative?

Dell'Acqua thinks one solution might be for organizations to create "Customized AI" tools that are specifically "tailored to ensure that human collaborators remain engaged in their tasks." Taking this step, he suggests, could be a good way to make sure people stay alert and involved.

My own approach, however, is somewhat different. We'll learn about it in the next chapter.

CHAPTER 11

Two-Question Minimum

If you have an infinite answer machine and the whole world has access to it—if you can be creative enough to imagine the right questions—you will have no end of opportunity.

—Claire Silver, "AI May Take Our Jobs—But Not Our Creativity"

One strategy I use to try to combat the concern identified in the previous chapter—that working with AI might cause people to go on intellectual autopilot—is to encourage my students (indeed *require* them) to pepper their AI tools with follow-up questions and instructions. I tell them that the best AI collaborations are energizing and dynamic. The experience should be like participating in a great class, leading a productive meeting, or simply having a stimulating conversation. AI tools should help your brain work better—not worse—than it normally would.

If you instead find yourself cognitively coasting whenever you interact with AI, you're probably doing something wrong. Or at least you're not getting as much out of these tools as you could.

So the next time you open up your chatbot of choice, try imposing on yourself something akin to the "Two-Drink Minimum" used by many comedy clubs and other entertainment venues—only in our case, we'll be imposing a "Two-Question Minimum."

In other words, when you first get a response from whatever chatbot you decide to use, probe it with at least two questions about the output it produced. They don't have to be brilliant questions. They don't have to be complex questions. They simply have to be questions. If you type some semicoherent words and put a question mark at the end, that counts, at least in the beginning. It's an intentionally low bar.

The point is simply to get you in the habit of something we've been stressing throughout this book. Take the "Chat" part of ChatGPT and other chatbots seriously. Have a conversation with them. Be an active part of the exchange, like a modern-day Socrates.

Don't mindlessly defer to the information and ideas it spits out. Verify its factual claims. Press on its reasoning. Operate with a vigilant, hard-to-fool mindset.

At the same time, however, try to be open to the possibility that interacting with these tools—particularly once you get a bit of practice—might lead to some valuable insights.

Take Ezra Klein of *The New York Times*, for example. Earlier in the book, we talked about the concerns Klein had with using AI to create the first draft of the writing he does. Here, as a reminder, is how he articulated his position:

> One way I think that A.I. could actually NOT make us more productive, more innovative, is that a lot of the innovation—a lot of the big insights—happen when we're doing the hard thing, when we're sitting there trying to figure out the first draft, or learn about a thing, or figure out what we're doing.

For this reason, he expressed a reluctance to turn to AI when initially working on a piece of writing. Yet he was much more enthusiastic about using it later on in the creative process, as a way to get some instantaneous—and he found quite perceptive—feedback on things he already wrote, including emails to people he deeply cares about: "So one of the things I will sometimes do, and did quite recently, is give the A.I. a series of personal documents, emails I wrote to people I love that were very descriptive of a particular moment in my life. And then I will ask the A.I. about them, or ask the A.I. to analyze me off of them."

The process, he continues, is "a little breathtaking. Almost every moment of true metaphysical shock (to use a term somebody else gave me) I've had here has been relational, at how good the A.I. can be—almost like a therapist, right? Sometimes it will see things, the thing I am not saying, in a letter, or in a personal problem. And it will zoom in there, right? It will give, I think, quicker and better feedback in an intuitive way that is not simply mimicking back what I said and is dealing with a very specific situation. It will do *better* than people I speak to in my life around that."

The tech journalist Casey Newton has been similarly impressed, if also a little unnerved, by the ability of various AI tools to give useful feedback. Here's how he described his experience on an episode of *Hard Fork*, a podcast he cohosts with another person we mentioned earlier in the book, Kevin Roose, the author of *Futureproof: 9 Rules for Surviving in the Age of AI*. "Increasingly, [these tools have] been able to identify the tone of how I'm writing about something," Newton shared. "And it's sort of asking me, did you mean it to sound this way? That is the eeriest part for me. . . . It feels like [AI] can get at the subtext of what I'm writing better than other things in the past."

To explain why he plans to keep using AI in this way, Newton added that "when you are a writer, that kind of feedback is a gift."

In the next chapter, we're going to try to use that gift, especially when it comes to a kind of writing that many of us spend a ton of time doing each day: emails.

CHAPTER 12

Finding Your Voice(s)

We routinely revise and rewrite our emails, memos, and even text messages. That behavior might seem like overkill, but the rewards are significant.

—Todd Rogers and Jessica Lasky-Fink, *Writing for Busy Readers*

Think of how many emails you have sent in the past week, the past month, the past year. Did you always strike the appropriate tone? Did you always use the right words? Did you consistently sound the way you intended?

In the rushed moments when messages are being drafted and hurriedly sent off, it is tough to stop and ask these kinds of questions, let alone answer them. But now you have the benefit of distance, as well as the chance to get some individualized feedback from AI.

Start by taking a look at some of your archived correspondence, from both your professional life and your personal one. Read a few aloud. Assess whether the voice you hear is the voice you want others to hear.

As I tell my students when we do this exercise in class, you shouldn't expect the tone, style, or even syntax in all of your emails to be consistent. If it were, I'd worry about your ability to develop the very important skill—particularly for lawyers and other advocates—of being able to customize your writing to meet the needs and expectations of different audiences. Persuasion, to borrow a phrase from the rhetorician Donald Bryant, involves adapting "ideas to people, and people to ideas."

If your messaging is monolithic, you're probably not going to get very far—with clients, with coworkers, with anybody.

Another way to think about this idea of having different voices is to consider an observation made by the psychologist and philosopher William James in a foundational book he published in 1890 called *The Principles of Psychology*: "A person has as many different social selves as there are distinct groups of persons about whose opinion he cares. He generally shows a different side of himself to each of these different groups. Many a youth who is demure enough before his parents and teachers swears and swaggers like a pirate among tough friends."

The multiplicity James describes is perhaps even more pronounced in email, a medium that allows you to craft what James calls your various "social selves" a bit more deliberately than does, say, spontaneous speech. You probably don't email your boss the same way you email your best friend. You probably don't email your siblings the same way you email your clients. Nor, I imagine, do you email your mom the same way you email your ex.

Think, too, of regional, international, and generational differences in communication norms and preferences. Books like *The Culture Map* by Erin Meyer highlight how tricky it can be to navigate between "high-context" cultures—where people communicate more indirectly, with lots of subtext and innuendo—and "low-context" cultures, where people tend to be more direct, even blunt. Cutting to the chase with someone who expects comments to be delivered with a certain amount of conversational finesse can come across as rude (or worse). And beating around the bush with a real straight shooter might cause the person to become impatient and annoyed. Neither mismatch is a great way to build collaborative rapport.

Is AI—and particularly its ability to rewrite things in many different styles—a panacea? Definitely not. An algorithm is no substitute for emotional intelligence and situational awareness. Yet as my students and I have found, it can be pretty good at both spotting patterns in the way you express yourself and suggesting alternatives.

In the next two AI Exercises, you'll have the opportunity to test out those capabilities for yourself.

AI Exercise #3
Tone Coach

Step 1: Find an email you have written that is over 150 words long.
Step 2: Copy and paste the email into the chatbot of your choice.
Step 3: Direct the chatbot to help you play around with the tone of the email. Shoot for 5-7 different styles. If you'd like, you

can choose a style based on the list below. It collects specific types of requests I have received from people who have asked me to help them craft particularly important emails.

- I want to sound less robotic.
- I want to sound less condescending.
- I want to sound less desperate.
- I want to sound more easy-breezy.
- I want to sound more confident.
- I want to sound more professional.
- I want to sound nice.
- I want to sound sincere.

The goal of these extra steps is not to encourage people to offload their email writing to AI. As Andrew Brodsky, a management professor at the University of Texas-Austin and the author of *Ping: The Secrets of Successful Virtual Communication*, has argued, there are real downsides to that strategy, particularly when corresponding with clients and coworkers. You could come across as inauthentic. You could signal that their thoughts are not worth your time. You could, fundamentally, miss out on an opportunity to establish a valuable human connection.

Instead, the AI part of the exercise is simply an additional way to get feedback—however flawed, incomplete, and even, at times, hallucinatory—on your current approach to email. "Something I do every day is when I'm writing an email to someone, I run my response through [ChatGPT] to check if I was passive-aggressive or snarky," said Conor Malloy, the project director of the Rentervention Initiative at the Law Center for Better Housing, on an episode of the Legal Service Corporation podcast *Talk Justice*. "I seek legitimate feedback to help refine the message before I send it out. This is the number one reason I use [AI] on a daily basis."

It's possible that inboxes all over the world might benefit if more people followed Malloy's lead.

AI Exercise #4
The Language of Common Life

The ideas were so big, and the language was so straightforward.

—Fei-Fei Li, *The Worlds I See: Curiosity, Exploration, and Discovery at the Dawn of AI*

Now that we've learned about the various roles AI can play when you are writing, let's think about how you might use the technology to help with another important aspect of advocacy: speaking.

The phrase that will orient our approach—the "language of common life"—is one I often use in my classes and workshops. I tell students about the American preacher Charles Grandison Finney, whose religious leadership during the first half of the 19th century earned him the title the "Father of Modern Revivalism." What helped make Finney so popular and effective was his commitment to speaking in what he called "the language of common life."

A helpful description of that approach appears in *The Evangelicals: The Struggle to Shape America* by the Pulitzer Prize–winning historian Frances FitzGerald: "[Finney] looked at people in the audience straight in the eye and addressed them as 'you.' His sentences were short and cogent, and his expressions colloquial."

Abraham Lincoln, one of the most revered US presidents of all time—and also a pretty darn good lawyer—is said to have operated in a similarly engaging manner. Here's how another Pulitzer Prize–winning historian, Doris Kearns Goodwin, in the book *Leadership in Turbulent Times*, captures Lincoln's approach: "The key to [Abraham] Lincoln's success [as a lawyer] was his uncanny ability to break down the most complex case or issue into its simplest elements. He never lost a jury by fumbling with or reading from a prepared argument, relying instead on his well-trained memory. He aimed for intimate conversations with the jurors, as if conversing with friends."

Both Lincoln and Finney seemed to understand several important things about skillfully holding people's attention:

1. Jargon can be off-putting.
2. Long, meandering sentences can tax people's patience.
3. Obscure references usually do more harm than good.

The "language of common life" is a much better, more audience-friendly technique.

Unfortunately, however, many of us have trouble adopting it. Listen to enough lawyers, policy makers, executives, and other advocates drone on and on—often through overly technical and complex terminology—and you'll realize that we often slip into the language of *pretentious* life, or the language of *condescending* life, or the language of *trying-to-sound* smart life. Perhaps AI can help.

Supercharged Thesaurus

One of the things that chatbots are really good at is rewording phrases, sentences, paragraphs, and even whole speeches. They're like supercharged thesauri, especially when you realize something important: You can ask chatbots for options that aren't necessarily more sophisticated and highfalutin (which is a mistake many people make when using a thesaurus) but rather options that simplify your message and target the goal of communicating in the language of common life.

The following instructions offer a way to help you do that.

Step 1: Find a speech, opening statement, or closing argument you have written. If you have never written one of those things, you can use a memo, brief, research paper, or some other document.

Step 2: Search the speech or document for examples of where you use the "language of common life." If you are looking for ideas, consider a compliment the chef Nigella Lawson gave Anthony Bourdain, whose food-focused books like *Kitchen Confidential*

and *Medium Raw* and television shows like *No Reservations* and *Parts Unknown* introduced millions of people to culinary cultures all around the world: "He's got that incredibly beautiful style when he talks. [It] ranges from erudite to brilliantly slangy."

You want to look for the "brilliantly slangy" part of Lawson's compliment. Here are some possibilities:

- Places where you use actual slang
- Places where you curse
- Places where you use an analogy that will appeal to a lot of people (It could be a sports analogy, a food analogy, a music analogy—anything that you think will resonate with your audience.)

Other options include:

- Places where you reference pop culture
- Places where you reference a local custom, celebrity, restaurant, landmark, or institution (Think, for example, of a commencement address that mentions a popular campus bar, legend, or tradition.)
- Places where you deliberately use folksy or at least unfancy language
- Places where you quote somebody using folksy or at least unfancy language

The goal isn't to fill an entire speech or conversation with the language of common life. But the complete absence of that language may be a sign that there is room to better connect with your intended audience. As Cate Stetson, a star appellate lawyer at the elite firm Hogan Lovells, has explained, you could be the smartest advocate in the world, but "unless you can turn around and talk to lay judges, [you're not going to get very far]."

Step 3: Use your chatbot of choice to help you add some "language of common life" to your speech or document. Here are a few options:

- Ask it to rewrite the speech or document—or certain parts of it—in the style of a comedian, television character, screenwriter, musician, podcaster, game show host, graphic novelist, politician, or other person you think effectively uses the language of common life.
- Ask it to rewrite the speech or document—or certain parts of it—in the style of a farmer, truck driver, bartender, cop, cowboy, mechanic, or butcher.
- Ask it to rewrite the speech or document—or certain parts of it—in the style of a place where you might expect to hear the language of common life: beauty parlor, barber shop, pub, diner, family barbecue, back porch, front stoop, locker room, beach, fishing boat, subway, or sporting event.

As with previous exercises, these steps are only suggestions and guidelines. Feel free to experiment a bit. Adapt the details to your particular circumstances, particularly if you don't give a lot of speeches or presentations but you do sometimes have to prepare for and navigate tricky conversations.

Here are examples of those conversations from a *Wall Street Journal* article that recommended role-playing with a chatbot as a way to help:

We all face conversations that we dread: summoning the courage to ask your boss for a raise, talking to your partner about prioritizing you over work, asking aging parents if they've saved enough for retirement. Using AI in this way for personal dilemmas can strengthen our arguments, illuminate our blind spots and turn tension into transformation.

We'll talk more about the benefits—and risks—of these types of AI collaborations in the next section of the book: "Time and Tasks."

PART 3

Time and Tasks

There is no reason to not want more help.

—Patrick Hebron, "Me, Myself, and AI"

CHAPTER 13

Quality Control

I could sit down and just be like, I'm thinking about writing a piece about X or here's a paragraph from the piece that I've just written. What am I missing? What am I forgetting?

—Steven Johnson, "Google's Hit A.I. Notebook and HatGPT"

Welcome to the third part of the book. I want to pick up where we left off in the second part, the one that dealt with "Communication and Creativity."

We ended that part by talking about an essay in *The Wall Street Journal* called "For Conversations You Dread, Try a Chatbot." Here are the opening lines: "Many people worry about the outsize role that AI may eventually play in our lives. But what if employing an AI program could actually help us with issues that cause fear and anxiety? We've found that it can be a surprisingly effective tool for figuring out how to approach emotionally charged conversations."

I bring up the essay again because of its practical focus on specific tasks where AI assistance might be useful. The essay describes a 75-year-old man who used AI to practice—and get feedback on—what he planned to say when suggesting to his 80-year-old sister that, because of her many health issues, she may need to enter an assisted living facility.

It also talks about someone who used AI to prep for a meeting where he would have to fire an employee and another person who used it to get similar help before a tense salary negotiation. "He had the AI role-play both his side of the conversation and his boss's side, with his 'boss' set at different levels of openness versus hostility to a raise," the article explained. "He found the program was able to remind him when he failed to highlight what could be mutually beneficial about a salary increase and when he failed to outline next steps. After all the practice, he reported that he was no longer nervous in carrying out the conversation."

Each of these examples highlights themes we've been stressing throughout the first two parts of the book. Treat chatbots and other generative AI tools as thought partners. Bounce ideas off them. Tap into their capacity to deliver frequent and immediate feedback, as well as their incredible range of personas, viewpoints, and alternative approaches to problems and projects.

The early models haven't really been reliable sources of facts. And given the probabilistic nature of the technology—the generated output is based on statistical predictions, not "ground truth"—there are real questions about just how accurate they can get. As Jeff Dean, a legendary software engineer at Google who has played an integral role in building the company's wide range of AI offerings, has explained, "These models are trained to predict plausible next tokens. . . . You can think of [a token] as a word or a piece of a word. And so when you predict plausible next tokens, that's a different thing than absolute truth, right? [What you are producing is] a probabilistically plausible sentence."

Yet for all their shortcomings, these tools can, with the right prompting, rapidly generate useful perspectives—and potentially even help you discover some of your own blind spots. For example, try giving your chatbot of choice the text of a project you're currently working on: a research memo, a business plan, an agenda for an upcoming meeting or conference. Then ask it, essentially, "What am I missing?"

Some of my students have used this technique to find holes in the logic of their arguments and improve the overall flow of their writing, especially if they prompt the chatbot to act as an expert in whatever subject they're covering, or as a really nitpicky grammarian, or even as the specific professor, judge, investor, or other kind of decision-maker they want to persuade.

Others have used it for more mundane tasks, sometimes taking advantage of the multimodal capabilities of AI to snap a picture of what they want feedback on instead of writing out a full list of items:

- Here's what I have packed for my spring break trip to Puerto Rico. What am I missing?
- Here's my budget for the three months I will be in Johannesburg this summer. What am I missing?

- Here's what I have bought for my four-year-old's birthday party. What am I missing?

The following AI exercise ("What Am I Missing?") offers an additional set of examples.

AI Exercise #5
What Am I Missing?

> Try to be one of those people on whom nothing is lost.
>
> —Henry James, *The Art of Fiction*

Background

The novel *The Other Americans* by Laila Lalami has received a lot of accolades. It was a finalist for the National Book Award, the California Book Award, and the Kirkus Prize. It won the Arab American Book Award and was shortlisted for the Aspen Literary Prize. It was also included on many Best Books of 2019 lists, including ones by *Time* magazine, *Variety*, the *New York Post*, and *The Washington Post*.

Part of the book's appeal is that the intricate details of the mysterious murder that drives the story are skillfully revealed through the voices and thoughts of many different characters: a jazz composer, a war veteran, a detective, the new (and old) owner of a bowling alley. But there is one voice in particular that really caught my attention, especially as I was putting together the materials for this book. It's the voice of the widow of the murder victim, right at the beginning of their relationship. "I have an eye for what other people miss," she says.

She's referring to her impressive ability to spot stylish and inexpensive clothes, but I soon started to think about the statement as a helpful way to capture one of the potentially useful things about artificial intelligence tools: They often have an eye for what people miss—in legal documents, in travel itineraries, in all kinds of things.

Assignment

Try using AI to ask the question "What am I missing?" The following list includes the examples we mentioned in the previous chapters as well as a few others. But you are certainly encouraged to come up with your own:

Travel: Here's what I have packed for my spring break trip to Puerto Rico. What am I missing?

Finance: Here's my budget for the three months I will be in Johannesburg this summer. What am I missing?

Family: Here's what I have bought for my four-year-old's birthday party. What am I missing?

Interview: Here's the list of questions I have prepared for the job applicant I am interviewing on Wednesday. What am I missing?

Contract: Here are the terms of the sublease I have drafted to rent out my apartment this semester. What am I missing?

Food: Here are the ingredients—and kitchen tools—I have to make brownies for my office tomorrow. What am I missing?

To get the best, most specific responses, you'll likely have to provide more details and context about your particular query. But this basic "What am I missing?" approach should at least give you a good structural start.

CHAPTER 14
Time-Savers

Technology can relieve us of routine work in order to give us time to focus on the more interesting parts of our work.

—Daniela Rus, director of the Computer Science and Artificial Intelligence Laboratory at MIT, quoted by Martin Ford in *Architects of Intelligence: The Truth About AI from the People Who Are Building It*

Eric Topol is a cardiologist and professor of molecular medicine who has held positions at the University of Michigan, the Cleveland Clinic, Case Western, and the Scripps Research Institute. In his book *Deep Medicine: How Artificial Intelligence Can Make Healthcare Human Again*, he offers a vision of AI collaboration in the medical world that might encourage anyone who thinks that something similar can happen in other professional domains (including law).

Topol is particularly interested in the ways that AI might help doctors spend less time on tasks that seem to get in the way of the kind of work we really want to do. "By freeing physicians from the tasks that interfere with human connection," Topol argues, "AI will create space for the real healing that takes place between a doctor who can listen and a patient who needs to be heard."

An article by Steve Lohr, the tech journalist we talked about in Chapter 6 ("Help or Hype?"), describes a physician who has begun to take advantage of these time-saving benefits: "Dr. Matthew Hitchcock, a family physician in Chattanooga, Tennessee, has an A.I. helper. It records patient visits on his smartphone and summarizes them for treatment plans and billing. He does some light editing of what the A.I. produces, and is done with his daily patient visit documentation in 20 minutes or so. Dr. Hitchcock used to spend up to two hours typing up these medical notes after his four children went to bed. 'That's a thing of the past,' he said. 'It's quite awesome.'"

A second example comes from a small town called Hermitage, Pennsylvania:

> Dr. Michelle Thompson, a family physician in Hermitage who specializes in lifestyle and integrative care, said the software had freed up nearly two hours in her day. Now, she has time to do a yoga class, or to linger over a sit-down family dinner. Another benefit has been to improve the experience of the patient visit, Dr. Thompson said. There is no longer typing, note-taking or other distractions. She

> simply asks patients for permission to record their conversation on her phone. "A.I. has allowed me, as a physician, to be 100 percent present for my patients," she said.

The idea that similar tools might allow lawyers and other advocates to be 100 percent present for their clients is partly why Carolyn Elefant, the author of *Solo by Choice*—a book about starting your own law firm—suggests that using "AI to transcribe an initial consultation or trial prep meeting is really a no-brainer." Her principal reason: "Recording a client meeting enables lawyers to focus on the client, without the distraction of taking notes."

She also highlights some additional benefits:

- "A transcript will always catch details that a notetaker will miss, sparing your office from costly and embarrassing repeated follow-up with your client."
- " AI-transcripts serve an educational function. If, for example, you explain how the divorce or incorporation process works during your initial client meeting, your client can consult the transcript to refer back to your instructions as you explained them."

In the article in which she identifies these benefits, "Can Lawyers Legally and Ethically Record Conversations with Clients Using Artificial Intelligence?," Elefant mentions several resources that can help you think through the privacy and confidentiality concerns that AI transcription tools raise. (For those interested, these resources include ABA Formal Opinion 01-422, Comment 18 to ABA Model Rule 1.6, and a law review article by John Bliss called "The Legal Ethics of Secret Client Recordings.") Along with making sure that you of course get the consent of your client before recording, you'll also want to carefully review the terms of service of whatever AI platform or products you decide to use. Here are three things Elefant says to avoid:

- Platforms or products that use the entirety of your recordings or transcriptions for training
- Platforms or products that retain information that you've uploaded even after you've deleted it
- Platforms that don't take reasonable steps to protect the privacy and confidentiality of your communications

Another sensible step—particularly if you take advantage of AI's ability to provide quick summaries of what gets recorded—is to check it for inaccuracies. In a story about how various businesses are using AI summaries of meetings to save their employees time and better document the topics discussed, the *Wall Street Journal* reporter Tom Dotan included a cautionary example. It involved a summary created by Microsoft's Copilot: "At one ad agency, a Copilot-generated summary of a meeting once said that 'Bob' spoke about 'product strategy.' The problem was that no one named Bob was on the call and no one spoke about product strategy."

At the same time, however, Dotan mentioned several success stories. Some people interviewed for the story "had already become reliant on Copilot if they were late to a meeting, to get a summary of what had been said. Those in different countries and time zones now have the option to skip meetings and read summaries." Art Hu, the global chief information officer at the consumer electronics company Lenovo, articulated the benefit in the following way: "[The tool] has allowed people to say 'You know what, there are already 10 other people on the call. I'm going to skip this one. I'm going to catch up in the morning by reading the digest and skipping to the parts of the meeting I really needed to hear.'"

CHAPTER 15

Meetings Magic

If you could send an assistant to attend your virtual meetings for you, would you? What about inviting one to take notes alongside you?

—Danielle Abril, "Can AI Summaries Save You from Endless Virtual Meetings?"

If you are new to using AI in meetings—whether with clients or coworkers—start with a very low-stakes setting. As Brian Chen, the author of the weekly "Tech Fix" column in *The New York Times*, warns, "Anything you do using an online service can potentially be seen by the company that runs it, whether it's a big tech company or an A.I. startup. So if your meeting covers sensitive topics like trade secrets or personnel issues, this may not be the best time to experiment with these new tools."

Begin instead with an informal conversation with a friend or family member—ideally someone who is also interested in experimenting with ways AI might help them save time and complete tasks. See how well the transcript produced by Zoom, Microsoft Teams, Google Meet, or some other video conferencing platform accurately captures not just what was said but, importantly, who said it.

We don't want to re-create the all-too-common phenomenon of somebody getting credit for an idea even though they simply repeated what another person already said. The physics professor Nicole Gugliucci helped highlight the role that gender can play in these situations when, in 2017, she posted the following note on social media, which quickly went viral: "My friends coined a word: 'hepeated.' For when a woman suggests an idea and it's ignored, but then a guy says the same thing and everyone loves it."

A more optimistic possibility is that using AI to record and analyze meetings might address these and other forms of bias. Think of the research conducted by Tonja Jacobi, a law professor and political scientist who has studied oral arguments in the United States Supreme Court. Jacobi found that "even though female Justices speak less often and use fewer words than male Justices, they are nonetheless interrupted during oral arguments at a significantly higher rate."

In a talk at New York University in 2021, Justice Sonia Sotomayor—whom Jacobi found to be the *most* interrupted justice at one point—said Jacobi's research contributed to the Court changing the format of oral arguments and its overall approach to asking questions: "[I] found that my colleagues are much more sensitive than they were before. You'll see us, even now, when we're speaking, a [justice] will say, 'I'm sorry, did I interrupt you?' That did not happen as much before."

Inconsiderate interruptions are one of the things that have pushed me to set up and review AI-generated transcripts and summaries of the courses I teach. Born into a family of fast-talking New Yorkers who don't always wait for you to finish your thoughts before they jump in with theirs, I know I have what the linguist Deborah Tannen calls a "high-involvement" conversation style. I nod. I comment. I interject—in ways that can be interpreted as impatient or rude. AI has helped me recognize and curb this tendency much more efficiently than I did before.

I've been recording my classes for years, but I used to have to watch an entire, say, two-hour video to spot the moments when I interrupted a student. Or I would have to rely on my imperfect memory to try to fast-forward to when those moments occurred. Now, with this virtually costless AI feature, I can simply—and very quickly—scan the transcripts of my classes and go right to the exchanges in which my interrupting habit might have been pedagogically unproductive. I can also much more systematically assess whether I interrupt certain students more than others, whether other students interrupt certain students more than others, and exactly how many students actually get to talk during the class (and for how long).

Before AI, I would have research assistants sit in the back of the room and mark down when each student raised their hand or got called on. My goal was to become more alert to potentially concerning patterns of participation. It is not really a group dialogue if one or two people monopolize the airtime.

But there were a few problems with giving my research assistants this task:

- First, their reports weren't always accurate. In a big, lively class, with a lot of rapid-fire questions and Socratic-style back-and-forth, it can be tough for even the most attentive research assistants to catalog every exchange.
- Second, their reports were incomplete. The research assistants could only tell me who spoke in class. They couldn't tell me for how long each student spoke. The AI recordings give me both of those pieces of information—and plenty more.

- Third (and perhaps most important), the research assistants didn't particularly enjoy this task, especially because it took time away from them contributing in other, more substantive and engaging ways.

I mention that last point—about the desirability of the task—because I think it is an important factor to consider when deciding what to delegate to AI, as I'll explain in the next chapter.

First, however, I want to stress that just because AI transcripts work for me doesn't mean they'll work for you. Recording classes has become an accepted norm at the law schools where I teach. So the students expect it, consent to it, and in many ways request it—especially when they may have to miss class or want to review a particular lesson.

But that might not be the case at your organization. Research by Rachel Schlund and Emily Zitek of Cornell University's School of Industrial and Labor Relations suggests when people perceive that AI is being used to monitor and evaluate their behavior, they complain more, they perform worse, and they report feeling like they have less autonomy—unless the technology is framed as a way for them to receive feedback designed to help them grow. "When artificial intelligence and other advanced technologies are implemented for developmental purposes, people like that they can learn from it and improve their performance," Zitek said in an interview after the research was published. "The problem occurs when they feel like an evaluation is happening automatically, straight from the data, and they're not able to contextualize it in any way."

The lesson: Using AI to support people seems like a much better organizational strategy than using AI to surveil them.

CHAPTER 16

Low-Hanging AI Fruit

Our study of 152 projects in almost as many companies reveals that highly ambitious moon shots are less likely to be successful than "low-hanging fruit" projects that enhance business processes.

—Thomas Davenport and Rajeev Ronanki,
"Artificial Intelligence for the Real World"

We mentioned in the previous chapter that the desirability of a task may be one factor to consider when deciding what tasks to try to delegate to AI. As Frances Frei—the Harvard Business School professor we learned about in Chapter 7—has suggested, a smart initial question to ask when trying to figure out which aspects of your job (or even your current To-Do list) could be offloaded to AI is, "Of all the things on my plate right now, what do I like the *least*?"

Remember that in Frei's role as a professor who writes books and articles, one of the things she likes least is having to constantly deal with a blank page. Here, as a reminder, is how she articulated that distaste: "I don't like the blank page. In fact, I will hide from the blank page and go to great lengths to avoid it."

Enter artificial intelligence—and specifically, ChatGPT. "ChatGPT means I never have a blank page. I can ask it a well-formulated question, and it gives me something. It's not great, but I'm not looking for great. I'm looking for a non-blank page, and then I get to riff off of that. And so it really empowers people like me that don't like to [create] the first draft."

I'm also a professor who writes books and articles. But I actually *love* blank pages. Getting to sit down at my desk every day and create something entirely new—an essay, a legal brief, the chapters in this book—is one of my favorite things about my job. So I don't really use AI to create first drafts.

Instead, I use it at the opposite end of the writing process. I use it to proofread—because that's the part of being a professor that *I* like the least. I don't enjoy looking for typos. I don't get a kick out of fixing formatting. Plus, I'm not very good at those things, especially compared to AI.

Which brings me to a second factor to consider when deciding what to try to delegate to AI: Is the task something AI is even good at?

In a contest between you and AI, are you better or is AI better? In other words, which of you has a competitive advantage?

To think about how our two factors—desirability and competitive advantage—fit together, it might be helpful to consider the following graph. On the y-axis we can put "Desirability." Tasks you really like to do go at the top. Tasks you really don't like to do head toward the bottom. Then on the x-axis we can put "Competitive Advantage."

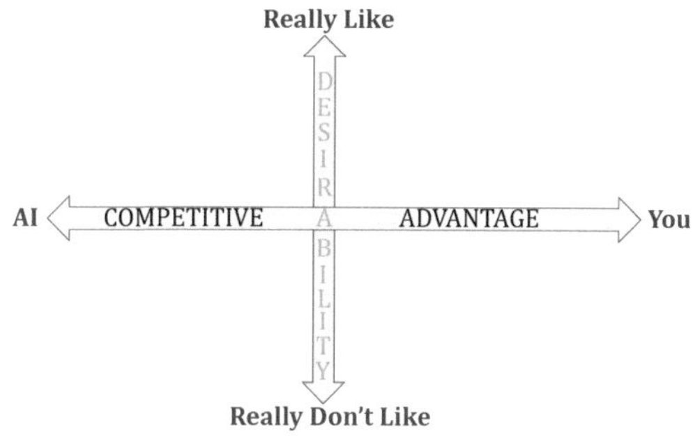

The farther to the right we move, the more *you* are better at the task than AI is. The farther to the left you go, the more *AI* is better at the task than you are. The sweet spot is the bottom left quadrant. Tasks you really don't like to do, and tasks that, compared to you, AI is really good at.

For Frances Frei, the sweet spot is effortlessly generating first drafts. For me, the sweet spot is proofreading. For the research assistants I asked to help me with my teaching, it was somewhat mindlessly—and quite monotonously—marking down the names of people I called on in class. And for the doctors we talked about in Chapter 14 ("Time-Savers"), it was typing their medical notes after each patient visit.

For you it might be something entirely different. Creating a workout schedule. Summarizing documents. Putting together the itinerary for a family trip, work retreat, or professional conference. One of my students even used ChatGPT to help her with what she found to be the extremely annoying parts of planning a wedding.

The point is to focus, at least initially, on what is essentially low-hanging AI fruit. We'll talk more about that strategy in the next chapter.

CHAPTER 17

A New World

For those people who enjoy learning and changing—and evolving how they work—this is a very exciting time.

—Aaron Levie, CEO of Box, "How to Build an AI-First Company"

We've been talking about using the twin factors of "desirability" and "competitive advantage" to target low-hanging AI fruit. An additional example from the world of medicine might be helpful, especially because a lot of the issues that health care workers face—burnout, time management, figuring out how to best allocate their mental and physical resources—apply to many other professionals as well.

The example comes from an article in *The New York Times* about how doctors have used AI to improve their bedside manner. The article highlighted the role that ChatGPT played in helping a team in the department of internal medicine at the University of Texas at Austin create a script that physicians could use to interact more compassionately with patients. "Doctors are famous for using language that is hard to understand or too advanced," said one of the leaders of the team, Dr. Christopher Moriates. So he was particularly excited to see that the version of the script that ChatGPT generated—especially after being prompted to address someone who lacks medical expertise and only reads at a fifth-grade level—was helpfully free of jargon. It even, in Dr. Moriates's view, came across as "more genuine" than what a typical doctor might produce. AI, in this task, had the advantage.

But as remarkable as it is to learn that a piece of software is capable of communicating sincerity, an underappreciated part of the story is that even though everyone on the Texas medical team was asked to create a script, none of them actually did. Whether because of too much work, too little sleep, or a combination of those and many other very human factors, the people specifically tasked with the assignment didn't complete it. Only ChatGPT ultimately delivered.

That difference in dependability is one of the biggest potential benefits of delegating tasks to AI. As we stressed in Chapter 4, ChatGPT and other AI tools are freakishly good at hitting deadlines.

Which helps explain why another doctor featured in the *New York Times* article, a rheumatologist in private practice in Dallas, said

ChatGPT had become his "constant companion": "He recently asked the program to write a letter of appeal to an insurer. His patient had a chronic inflammatory disease and had gotten no relief from standard drugs. Dr. Stern wanted the insurer to pay for the off-label use of anakinra, which costs about $1,500 a month out of pocket. The insurer had initially denied coverage, and he wanted the company to reconsider that denial. It was the sort of letter that would take a few hours of Dr. Stern's time but took ChatGPT just minutes to produce."

The result: "After receiving the bot's letter, the insurer granted the request. 'It's like a new world,' Dr. Stern said."

Dr. Gregory Moore, a radiologist who has held executive positions in the health science divisions at Google and Microsoft and also taught at Stanford Medical School, was similarly impressed. "'I wish I would have had this [technology] when I was in training,' he said. 'I have never seen or had a coach like this.'"

He was particularly struck by how well ChatGPT responded when he asked it to help him figure out what to say to a friend who had recently been diagnosed with an advanced form of cancer for which the outlook was unfortunately very bleak. "The program gave him the words to explain to his friend the lack of effective treatments. . . . It also suggested ways to break bad news when his friend asked if she would be able to attend an event in two years."

Not every physician, though, is as sanguine about the help AI can provide. Dr. Dev Dash, a professor of emergency medicine who did a postdoc in Stanford's Center for Artificial Intelligence in Medicine and Imaging, told the same reporter who spoke with the other doctors we've mentioned that, so far, he's been "underwhelmed" by the assistance ChatGPT and other large language models can provide doctors: "In tests performed by Dr. Dash and his colleagues, they received replies that occasionally were wrong but, he said, more often were not useful or were inconsistent. If a doctor is using a chatbot to help communicate with a patient, errors could make a difficult situation worse."

"'I know physicians are using this [technology],'" Dr. Dash added. "'I've heard of residents using it to guide clinical decision-making. I don't think it's appropriate.'"

Similar concerns—but for lawyers—can be found in the formal guidance on AI offered by the American Bar Association's Standing Committee on Ethics and Professional Responsibility. Here's a sample of the questions they encourage attorneys of all kinds to consider when deciding whether to collaborate with (and delegate tasks to) generative artificial intelligence tools, which the committee refers to as "GAI tools":

- What level of competency should lawyers acquire regarding a GAI tool?
- How can lawyers satisfy their duty of confidentiality when using a GAI tool that requires input of information relating to a representation?
- When must lawyers disclose their use of a GAI tool to clients?
- What level of review of a GAI tool's process or output is necessary?
- What constitutes a reasonable fee or expense when lawyers use a GAI tool to provide legal services to clients?

In many ways, the committee's position is one that often surfaces when powerful new technologies emerge: Just because you *can* use AI to help you with various tasks doesn't mean you should—or at least not without carefully reflecting on the professional and ethical implications of your actions.

You don't want to ultimately regret asking AI to do something you should have done yourself, an outcome we will learn more about in the next chapter when we discuss a potential risk when delegating tasks to AI: later feeling a sense of "delegation remorse."

CHAPTER 18

Delegation Remorse

Although at first I wanted to skip the tedium and delegate data operations to an undergraduate to do the essential yet undervalued and underpaid work, the process of labeling the dataset myself by hand provided its own insights.

—Joy Buolamwini, *Unmasking AI*

I suspect that the lawyers who have notoriously had ChatGPT write a brief for them and then failed to check whether the cases it cited were actually real have a bit of delegation remorse. I also suspect that the school administrators we talked about in Chapter 8—the ones who were harshly criticized for relying on ChatGPT to craft what was supposed to be a supportive, psychologically sensitive email to students soon after a traumatic school shooting—have a bit of delegation remorse.

The same is likely true of the companies described in an article published in *Forbes* under the headline "AI-Generated Employee Handbooks Are Causing Mayhem at the Companies That Use Them":

> Companies are increasingly turning to AI to generate important, often legally binding, employment documents—from company handbooks and workplace policies to contracts like offer letters and separation agreements, according to interviews with four HR and payroll service providers. And in several cases, these documents, spun using AI tools like ChatGPT, overlook key clauses and crucial issues putting employers at serious legal and financial risk.

A particularly costly AI oversight involved not including anything about an overtime policy:

> One California-based firm with 200 employees used AI to generate their company handbook, Daniel Grace, a director at global HR service provider Iris Software Group, told *Forbes*. But after distributing it company wide, managers discovered it didn't include an overtime policy, a legal requirement in the state. When employees worked several hours in overtime, the company was hit with a massive and unexpected wage bill. "They went back to look at the handbook and there was a section on overtime in there, but it was blank," Grace said.

Another AI oversight, in a different company, surfaced in a severance agreement, the document that lays out the terms of an employee's termination from their job:

> In the UK, an HR team used Microsoft Bing's AI copilot to produce a severance agreement, Grace said. The legally binding document, which omitted essential information, was then sent to the employee's legal counsel. "Their lawyer essentially just threw it out the window and said this is useless. It really tarnished their own negotiation, and they ended up having to pay a higher settlement amount."

These AI blunders remind me of an admonition from the computational linguist Emily Bender. "If your work is actually meaningful," she said, "you don't want to start with ChatGPT output." Headed into court to defend someone who is facing a life sentence? Probably not a good time to experiment with having ChatGPT craft your opening statement. About to make a big presentation to some important investors, donors, or internal stakeholders? Don't rely on an AI image generator to put together your entire slide deck.

Remember one of the major themes of this book: Treat AI tools, especially at first, like they are energetic (but often erratic) interns. Don't give them anything important, at least not without closely monitoring—and being ready to substantially revise—whatever they produce. They are, in the words of one team of AI researchers and forecasters, sort of like "a scatterbrained employee who thrives under careful management."

The *Forbes* article on AI-generated employee handbooks is again instructive. "Let's face it," one of the human resources experts interviewed said. "People are using artificial intelligence tools to speed things up, and they really shouldn't. These things have teething issues. They're generating these documents. No one's proofreading them, they're publishing them, and it's causing more issues than it would have caused if they'd taken the time to make the handbook successfully in the first instance."

In the next chapter, we'll talk about a different kind of delegation remorse, with the help of some useful insights from the economist Steve Levitt and the political scientist Virginia Eubanks.

CHAPTER 19
Automating Inequality

What if automating only increases efficiencies in an already imperfect system?

—Amanda Lenhart, "How Algorithms Can Punish the Poor"

We've talked about how the sweet spot for delegating tasks to AI—and for protecting yourself against delegation remorse—can be found by taking our delegation matrix and targeting the sweet spot in the bottom left corner.

What you want are tasks that (1) you really don't like to do and (2) AI is really good at.

A study called "When and How Artificial Intelligence Augments Employee Creativity," published in the *Academy of Management Journal* by a team of business professors, for example, presents evidence that using AI to handle some of the more boring and repetitive tasks of being a salesperson had a number of positive effects, especially for the higher-skilled salespeople who participated:

- It boosted morale.
- It improved the salespeople's mood.
- It gave them a chance to focus on issues that required more creative problem-solving.

As Kartik Hosanagar, a professor of technology and digital business at Penn, has suggested, one of the most exciting things about AI is the possibility that it will "allow us to outsource the 'grunt work' to AI," leaving people with more time to concentrate on the parts of their job that are more engaging. In his view, the chance for humans to collaborate with AI in this and other capacities will lead to "the biggest boost in productivity we have ever seen."

Yet as the economist Steve Levitt has observed of his own efforts to use delegation as a way to enhance his productivity, there is a risk that, in the interest of efficiency and growth, you might mistakenly offload the parts of your job or project that you actually enjoy the most.

The example Levitt offers predates ChatGPT and other advances in artificial intelligence, but I still think it provides a helpful cautionary tale, especially as AI-powered tools continue to expand and improve the delegation options for each of us. "When I was getting started as a grad student, I did every aspect of a project," Levitt explained on an episode of his podcast *People I (Mostly) Admire.* "I came up with the idea, I typed in the data, I cleaned and analyzed the data, I made tables and figures, and I did the writing." It was very time consuming. But it was also, to Levitt, extremely rewarding.

Eventually, however, Levitt got access to bigger research budgets and the opportunity to hire smart, capable people to help him—sort of like how now, thanks to AI, we all have the opportunity to assemble a seemingly endless supply of digital assistants. Levitt no longer needed to (and in many ways couldn't) do everything on his own. So he started delegating.

He began with the task that, administratively, seemed like the easiest thing to assign to somebody else: analyzing data.

The problem (or as Levitt put it in the podcast, the "sad irony") is that Levitt really loves analyzing data. It's his favorite part of doing research. As Stephen Dubner, who cowrote the bestselling *Freakonomics* series of books with Levitt, observed all the way back in 2003, well before their first book together was published, "Levitt will tell you that all he does is sit at his desk, day and night, wrestling with some strange mountain of data. He will tell you that he would do it for free, and you tend to believe him."

But once Levitt started delegating, he gave that part of his job away, a decision he now regrets. "I ended up delegating away what I loved in pursuit of higher productivity," he explained. "And in the end, I was productive, but honestly all the fun went out of it, and I soured on academic research."

It would be incredibly sad if a drive for AI-assisted hyperefficiency ultimately caused you to experience a similar disenchantment, not specifically with academic research, but with the particular work and other activities you find meaningful. Worse still, what if somebody else's drive for AI-assisted hyperefficiency emotionally empties you in that way? Or if larger political and market forces do?

Think back to the critique by Molly Crabapple in the "Picture This" exercise that involved AI image generators. Expressing her frustration at the risk that work would be taken away from professional human illustrators and given to environmentally costly software, she said, "I truly don't understand why anyone would decide to burn tons and tons and tons of carbon for the sole purpose of stealing a job that people love to do."

Or consider the social workers described in *Automating Inequality: How High-Tech Tools Profile, Police, and Punish the Poor* by Virginia Eubanks. A new system designed to streamline how low-income families and individuals in the state of Indiana receive welfare benefits ended up depersonalizing the entire process: "The old system involved caseworkers developing one-on-one relationships with individuals and families and following cases through to completion. The new system was 'self-serve,' technology-focused, and presented call center workers with a list of tasks to complete rather than a docket of families to serve. No one worker had oversight of a case from beginning to end; when clients called the 1-800 number, they always spoke to a new worker. Because the [people in charge] saw relationships between caseworkers and clients as invitations to fraud, the system was designed to sever those links."

The new system created so many problems that the Indiana governor at the time ultimately canceled the $1.3 billion contract under which it operated, just 3 years into what was supposed to be a 10-year arrangement. But perhaps two bigger lessons come from the frustrating experience of the social workers who were forced to hand over key parts of their job to an algorithm:

- First, delegation remorse can be even worse when it is externally imposed.
- Second, as a very perceptive book review of *Automating Inequality* put it, "Everyone needs to understand that technology is no substitute for justice."

CHAPTER 20

Four Thousand Weeks

How did it get so late so soon?
It's night before it's afternoon.
December is here before it's June.
My goodness how the time has flewn.
How did it get so late so soon?

—Dr. Seuss, "How Did It Get Late So Soon?"

In *Four Thousand Weeks: Time Management for Mortals*, the journalist Oliver Burkeman suggests that "the real measure of any time management technique is whether or not it helps you neglect the right things." Burkeman's book is a helpful reminder that, as both its first page and last page emphasize, "the average human lifespan is absurdly, terrifyingly, insultingly short." We get, if we're lucky, around 4,000 weeks, which is why Burkeman picked that number for the title of his book.

That's not a lot of time. So I am incredibly grateful that you have decided to spend at least a little of your 4,000 weeks with the first three sections of this book, and I certainly hope you continue onto the fourth (and final) section as well: "Learning and Leading."

Writing it was something I really enjoyed—and definitely didn't delegate to a chatbot.

PART 4

Learning and Leading

Computers give us, for the first time, the choice of deciding whether we want to produce role-learning people who do disciplined routine work and follow orders, or whether we want to produce critical, creative minds.

—Seymour Papert, former codirector of the MIT Artificial Intelligence Laboratory and Professor of Education

CHAPTER 21

Producing More, Understanding Less

It is going to take us a little while to figure out how to redo pedagogy.

—Matthew Bidwell, "AI in Human Resources"

We ended the previous section by grappling with the problem of delegation remorse—that feeling of regret that comes when you realize that the task, assignment, or activity you delegated away is actually something you wish you could keep doing. The initial example we used came from the economist Steve Levitt, the coauthor of *Freakonomics* and a past recipient of the prestigious Clark Medal, which is given to the top American economist under the age of 40. Here's a reminder of how Levitt articulated the delegation remorse he experienced after he, in an effort to become more efficient as a scholar, began to delegate to his research assistants the extremely time consuming—but also, to him, very joy-producing—task of data analysis: "I ended up delegating away what I loved in pursuit of higher productivity. And in the end, I was productive, but honestly all the fun went out of it, and I soured on academic research."

A related concern comes in the paper by the anthropologist Lisa Messeri and the neuroscientist Molly Crockett we mentioned in Chapter 6 ("Help or Hype?"). They're the ones who worry that an overdependence on AI, particularly among scientists, might lead us to a world in which we "produce more but understand less."

Messeri and Crockett are not AI doomers. Early on in the paper—which was published in the journal *Nature* under the title "Artificial Intelligence and Illusions of Understanding in Scientific Research"—they make clear that they "do not take the position that AI should never be used in scientific research." And soon after the paper was released, Crockett—who specializes in machine learning and natural language processing—told a reporter at the science magazine *Ars Technica* that "I have used AI in my work, and I'm really excited about its potential."

Yet both Crockett and Messeri nevertheless worry about what may happen should "AI-assisted research come to dominate the production of scientific knowledge." One of their particular fears is a situation where, because of the seductive convenience and efficiency of AI tools, *more* and *more* people rely on these tools for *more* and *more* of the research process: reading, summarizing, and analyzing existing data and information; generating new ideas and hypotheses; describing, editing, and disseminating findings.

This intellectual homogenization might result in a scientific monoculture that lacks crucial elements of creativity and diversity and is "vulnerable to error, bias, and missed opportunities for innovation." In other words, if everybody uses the same coauthor—and cobrainstormer and coeditor—we could find ourselves with a dangerously narrow, stagnant, and incomplete understanding of the world.

Messeri and Crockett's misgivings may remind you of a few of the red flags raised by somebody else we talked about earlier in the book: the Wharton business professor Ethan Mollick, who authored the book *Co-Intelligence: Living and Working with AI.* Here, as a review, is how Mollick explained the risk that AI's alluring ease might have a stifling effect on invention and original thinking:

> The implications of having AI write our first drafts (even if we do the work ourselves, which is not a given) are huge. One consequence is that we could lose our creativity and originality. When we use AI to generate our first drafts, we tend to anchor on the first idea that the machine produces, which influences our future work. Even if we rewrite the drafts completely, they will still be tainted by the AI's influence.

We described this process as a kind of "path dependence," where starting out in a certain direction constrains the next moves you might decide to take. If we rely on AI to set our initial menu of options, we might limit ourselves to choosing from whatever is on that menu and miss out on exploring potentially more useful insights, perspectives, and solutions. A lot of innovation comes from starting from scratch.

We'll want to continue to consider the problem of path dependence—and the concern about "producing more but understanding less"—throughout the rest of this book, particularly now that we are about to turn our attention to the role AI may have (and already has had) in education and professional training.

AI and Education

How should teachers approach AI? How should students approach AI? How about the leaders of businesses, government agencies, and nonprofit organizations, all of whom know that a key driver of success is making sure their employees have the skills necessary to thrive in a fast-changing world?

Many, like Sal Khan, the founder of the online education powerhouse Khan Academy, are incredibly optimistic about AI. In *Brave New Words: How AI Will Revolutionize Education (and Why That's a Good Thing)*, he details how Khan Academy has used AI to create a platform that "offers every person an opportunity to engage deeply in the education process in entirely new ways. Among other things, it provides a personalized and patient tutor that focuses on the learner's interests or struggles and empowers educators to better understand how they can fully support their students."

Others, like Dan Meyer, who earned his doctorate in math education from Stanford and later became the chief academic officer of the online learning company Desmos, are more apprehensive, particularly when it comes to chatbot pedagogy. "Generative AI is best," he has written, "at what something teachers need least"—namely, personalizing the text of a word problem to fit a student's interests.

Meyer then cites multiple studies that suggest that this kind of superficial intervention—where, for instance, the math questions given to a student who likes basketball will include examples about basketball and the math questions given to a student who likes puppies will include examples about puppies—doesn't really work that well. "The larger issue here," he explains, "is that technologists are building towards AI's *strengths* rather than teacher and learner *needs*."

You'll get to engage with these and other perspectives throughout the rest of this book, beginning with a suggestion I try to make whenever I talk about artificial intelligence with students, lawyers, teachers, administrators, government officials, and pretty much everyone else: AI, when used well, can be an incredible "feedback machine."

CHAPTER 22

Feedback Machines

Outside of an annual review, most people usually get no feedback on their day-to-day efforts.

—Daniel Goleman, "Leadership That Gets Results"

Think of a time when you could have really used some immediate feedback—on a document you've drafted, on a speech you've prepared, on everything from a big project at work, to a small project at school, to a side project you've been trying to cram into your free nights and weekends. Waiting for your next performance review isn't really an option. Or at least it's not an ideal one. Nor is hoping to secure some quality one-on-one time with your boss, teacher, or client. You want to know, *now*, what you can do to improve.

One of the most promising educational aspects of artificial intelligence tools is their capacity to provide this type of instant guidance. When skillfully used, they can be tremendously valuable "feedback machines."

You don't have to worry about AI being too busy or distracted to get back to you. You don't have to worry about AI being annoyed or judgmental. It will immediately (and quite supportively) respond to your requests, particularly if you direct it with specific, context-rich instructions.

A key part of the process is to not be intimidated by the black-box mystique that often surrounds AI. "When I talk to people about artificial intelligence," observes Helen Toner, the director of strategy at Georgetown's Center for Security and Emerging Technology and a former board member at OpenAI, "what I hear a lot from non-experts is 'I don't understand AI.' But when I talk to experts, a funny thing happens: They say, 'I don't understand AI, and neither does anyone else.'"

Toner is right to point out that this dual befuddlement among AI novices and AI experts represents "a strange set of affairs." She's also right, however, when she says that "AI can be confusing, but it's not magical. There are some parts of AI systems we do already understand well, and even the parts we don't understand won't be opaque forever."

She then adds that "when it comes to those building the technology, technologists sometimes act as though if you're not elbows deep in the technical details, then you're not entitled to an opinion on what we should do with it. Expertise has its place, of course, but history shows us how important it is that the people affected by a new technology get to play a role in shaping how we use it. Like the factory workers in the 20th century who fought for factory safety, or the disability advocates who made sure the world wide web was accessible. You don't have to be a scientist or engineer to have a voice."

That last statement—you don't have to be a scientist or engineer to have a voice in the conversation about AI—deserves special attention. Whether you are a teacher or a student, an executive or an intern, a parent or a child, you have a voice in the role AI will play in your life. AI is one of those subjects where we need the curriculum to be coproduced.

Fortunately, we are all well suited for this kind of collaboration. I've mentioned that AI tools can be incredible feedback machines. But so can human beings. We comment. We critique. We share our thoughts, insights, and frustrations.

So in the next chapter, we'll take a look at some of the feedback that has been specifically directed at various AI classroom interventions.

CHAPTER 23

F**k the Algorithm

This incident has shone the media spotlight on the question of AI bias.

—Daan Kolkman, "What the World Can Learn from the UK's A-Level Grading Fiasco"

Some of the loudest—and, shall we say, most *colorful*—feedback about AI interventions in education came in August of 2020, outside the British Department for Education in central London. Hundreds of high school students gathered to protest the government's decision to use a predictive algorithm to assign grades to university hopefuls throughout the United Kingdom, when, because of the COVID-19 pandemic, the all-important "A-Level" exams that are typically used to determine who gets into which school were canceled.

For a parallel in the United States education system, think of the outrage that would result if instead of actually taking the SAT, ACT, or any of their AP exams, high school students around the country simply received a score generated by an algorithm that *guessed* what grade they'd each probably receive based on a bunch of factors like school size and the district's past performance that, many claimed in the British example, penalized students from smaller, less-resourced schools.

Here's how Louise Amoore, the author of *Cloud Ethics: Algorithms and the Attributes of Ourselves and Others*, described the situation in an essay published soon after the details of the fiasco were revealed:

> An improbable nightmare that stalked students in the past was tearing open an envelope to find someone else's exam results inside. On August 13, for tens of thousands of A-level students in England, this became a reality. The predictive algorithm developed by the qualifications regulator Ofqual disregarded the hard work of many young people in a process that ascribed weight to the past performance of schools and colleges. As one teenager described

> the experience of being downgraded: "I logged on at 8am and just started sobbing."

The students who gathered outside the Department of Education in London were more blunt: "Fuck the Algorithm!" they chanted, while some held up signs that said things like "Your Algorithm Doesn't Know Me" and "Give Me Back My Grades." The public support for the students was so intense and the overall scrutiny of the system so widespread that, within days, education officials changed their position and decided to throw out the grades the algorithm generated.

Having that kind of engaged, "critical audience" is crucial if we want to avoid similar AI blunders in the future, according to the computational sociologist Daan Kolkman. In an article about AI bias called "What the World Can Learn from the UK's A-Level Grading Fiasco," Kolkman suggests that "without a critical audience that opposes algorithms and points out their shortcomings, we will keep hearing about the occasional incident with automated decision making, but never learn of the majority of algorithms [whose] screw-ups never see the light of day."

Kolkman recognizes that developing those audiences raises its own set of concerns:

- Do we appoint algorithm regulators?
- How would those regulators deal with proprietary systems?
- Who would pay for the high costs of monitoring and regular audits?
- How would the regulators even find where algorithms are used?

The answers to these questions may depend on whether the educational context is a high school, a university, or a workforce training program. But Kolkman is convinced that they have become increasingly important to ask. "If public officials everywhere don't start to think more seriously about fostering critical audiences for algorithms, I'm afraid we'll hear, 'F**k the algorithm!' far more often in the future."

In the next chapter, we'll turn our attention to a much different set of voices, including some teachers, students, and professional development specialists, whose position isn't "F**k the algorithm" but more like "God bless the algorithm."

CHAPTER 24

God Bless the Algorithm

"Does this [AI tool] make my life easier? Yes," said high-school history teacher Richard Vanden Bosch. "But that's not what this is about. It's about making the students better writers."

—Sara Randazzo, "That Essay Got a B+. An AI Bot Graded It."

The data scientist Rumman Chowdhury is the founder and CEO of Humane Intelligence, a nonprofit organization designed to provide the kind of AI auditing and evaluations that we highlighted in the previous chapter, when we learned about the A-Level scandal in the UK and Daan Kolkman's suggestions that, to avoid future ones, we need to develop "critical audiences" of oversight.

In a talk called "Your Right to Repair AI Systems," Chowdhury captured a disheartening sentiment probably shared not just by the students affected by the A-Level scandal—or the ones who went through something similar with a grade-producing algorithm for the International Baccalaureate that year—but by a much larger group of AI-weary folks. "I've talked to hundreds of people over the last few years," she explained. "Architects and scientists, journalists and photographers, rideshare drivers and doctors, and they all say the same thing. People feel like an afterthought."

She went on to say that people "know that their data is harvested often without their permission to create these sophisticated systems. They know that these systems are determining their life opportunities. They also know that nobody ever bothered to ask them how the system should be built, and they certainly have no idea where to go if something goes wrong."

These concerns are certainly important to keep in mind. But so is the enthusiasm expressed by the many teachers, students, administrators, and professional development executives who have started to experiment with AI and consider it to be a tremendously exciting educational tool. We have already mentioned the book *Brave New Words* by Sal Khan, and it is worth sharing some of the AI success stories he includes.

One comes from Peggy Buffington, the superintendent in a small city in Indiana called Hobart. Her school district was among the first in the United States to use Khanmigo, the AI-powered tutoring chatbot Khan and his team developed in collaboration with OpenAI: "After [the schools in Hobart] employed the AI for six months, the biggest gains they saw in their students were in the sphere of self-confidence, which is traditionally very difficult to address in a classroom setting. 'Student achievement has to start with confidence within themselves, confidence that comes with the knowledge that they know that they can do it,' [Buffington] tells me. 'Our job is to make sure that we are equipping our students with a confidence level in their abilities. The AI is a game changer here.'"

Khan then adds that "Buffington has seen these gains manifest themselves most plainly when watching the level of engagement increase amongst students in classrooms that have worked with Khanmigo. 'Where students were once uncomfortable raising their hands in class to ask questions, they are far less afraid to ask the AI tutor questions,' she says. 'Talking to an AI tutor eliminated the specter of public shame or anxiety. It's making them more engaged, and they love the responses they get from the AI. They come to school, and they feel confident in their work.'"

Support for this view can be found in a *Wall Street Journal* article that looked at various efforts to use AI to ease the grading burden of teachers and increase the speed and frequency with which students receive feedback:

> Incoming high-school senior Isaiah Green in California's Central Valley said he grew to love the use of [AI] in his Advanced

> Placement U.S. History class. He credits the [algorithmic] grader with giving him confidence when he walked into the AP exam in the spring, because he'd spent weeks getting instant feedback after completing timed essay prompts.

Imagine if you approach your next work assignment or personal project with that kind of confidence, because you spent weeks getting instant feedback on everything from the logic of your arguments, to the persuasiveness of your examples, to the originality of your ideas.

Feedback has been called the "ultimate human growth hormone" because of the way it can supercharge people's academic and professional development. Yet in many environments—especially once you enter the workforce—feedback is an incredibly scarce resource. People don't always have time to give it. People don't always know how to give it. Many of us are often even reluctant to ask for it.

One of the big promises of AI is that it may be able to help address some of these feedback deficits. Which is why, throughout this book, we've been exploring various feedback-focused ways to use AI tools. In the "Title Search" exercise, we talked about using AI to get feedback on the titles you put on papers, blogs, articles, and other pieces of writing. In "Tone Coach" and "The Language of Common Life," we talked about using AI to get feedback on your emails and speaking style. And in "What Am I Missing?" we talked about using AI to get feedback on things as different as the structure of your reasoning, the accuracy of your projected budgets, and even what you might need to pack for a long-overdue vacation.

The next section will describe an additional AI feedback exercise that might be worth trying: "Half-Life Your Message."

AI Exercise #6
Half-Life Your Message

> The one thing [Oliver Wendell Holmes] didn't like about [being a judge] was the tediousness of lawyers. "Dear me. Hardly anyone knows how to argue a case," he confided to Mrs. Gray. "You can twig in one minute what a man will take five to fifteen minutes to utter with due rhetorical emphasis."
>
> —Stephen Budiansky, *Oliver Wendell Holmes: A Life in War, Law, and Ideas*

I sometimes get asked by organizations to design training workshops for their employees. A pretty common request is for programs that help people become more concise, compelling communicators. No organization, for example, has ever asked me, "Is there any way you can teach our staff to write *longer*, more rambling emails?" Or "Can you show people how to drone on and on while giving a presentation or running a meeting?"

What folks want are ways to tighten and trim the sentences, slogans, and paragraphs they send out into the world. Few people's reaction to a memo or speech is "You know what that could have used? More words!"

So something I have recently tried is an AI-enhanced version of an intriguing feedback exercise developed by a team of public health researchers at the University of Michigan: Elyse Aurbach, Katherine Prater, Brandon Patterson, and Brian Zikmund-Fisher. Called "Half-Life Your Message," the exercise is designed to help you discover and prioritize the core message of whatever you are trying to communicate. "In our experience," the researchers explain, "learners and practitioners of Half-Life Your Message take away many lessons from the activity. Most discover that they can express their main point in less time than they originally thought.

Many also experience an 'ah ha' moment when they uncover an unexpected central message or discover that they need to start their argument from a different place than they originally thought."

With those benefits in mind, here are the instructions I give at the beginning of the exercise, before I add my AI modification:

Step 1: Pick a case you are working on, a paper you are writing, or some other substantial project on your To-Do list.

Step 2: Record yourself trying to explain the value of the project in 60 seconds. Some questions to consider:

- What background knowledge will you need to provide your audience for them to understand the value of your project?
- What is the most interesting, novel, or important aspect of your project?
- If your audience only takes away two insights from your 60-second explanation, what do you want those two things to be? How about if they only take away one insight?

Step 3: Record yourself trying to explain the value of the project again—but this time you only get 30 seconds.

Step 4: Cut the recording time to 15 seconds.

Step 5: Cut it to 7.5 seconds.

Step 6: Write down 2–3 sentences that identify (a) the version of the recording—60 seconds, 30 seconds, 15 seconds, 7.5 seconds—that you think is the most effective and (b) the reasons for your choice.

Now comes the AI component. It wasn't included in the original exercise the public health researchers developed. If it doesn't work for you, blame me—not them.

I have, however, had a lot of success with it when working with my students and putting on professional development trainings. So I hope you'll at least give it a shot. The basic idea is to take advantage of the following two characteristics of ChatGPT and other chatbots:

- They are really good at rapidly giving you multiple ways to condense and rephrase the sentences and paragraphs you feed them.
- They are helpfully—and oftentimes quite cheerily—ruthless.

In other words, chatbots don't care that you may have spent the last several days, weeks, or even months toiling away at a certain document or speech. Ask them to cut your memo, book, chapter, or wedding toast in half, and they will immediately comply—with all the remorse of a guillotine.

They won't show any compunction for all the time, effort, and angst you have invested in your current draft. Nor will they mourn anything they decide to jettison. Sunk costs are not something that chatbots fret over. Instead, they'll dutifully, if mercilessly, reduce your message by whatever amount you suggest.

I've been focusing on 50 percent reductions to keep in line with the "Half-Life Your Message" theme of the original exercise. But you're certainly not bound by that number. Consider, for example, the following sample prompts and approaches:

- **One:** "Here's an email I need to send about a change in our office's work-from-home policy. Create four different versions. Each should be 10 percent shorter than the current one—but don't make any changes to the final paragraph. The information there is very important, and I really like the way the last two lines are worded."
- **Two:** "I have been asked to appear on a three-person panel at a conference next week. I've been told I'll have five minutes to make some opening remarks before the broader discussion begins. But I'm worried that if the panel starts late or the other two people use more than their allotted time, I may only get two or three minutes. So please come up with a two-minute option and a three-minute option. Here's the five-minute version I have so far."

In a biography of the US Supreme Court Justice Oliver Wendell Holmes Jr., Stephen Budiansky praises Holmes for the elegant economy of his communication style: "No one knew how to strip off excess judicial verbal poundage better than Holmes."

Budiansky adds that the esteemed federal court judge Learned Hand—no slouch himself in the clarity and concision department—revered Holmes for having "a 'matchless gift of compression,' an ability to reduce an idea to its essence as did a great poet."

Few of us have that same ability, at least unassisted. But maybe with the right kind of AI feedback (and halflife-ing) we can get a little closer to the Holmesian ideal, both when we write and when we speak. "For one thing," Budiansky notes, "[Holmes] almost completely avoided legal jargon and cant phrases in his judicial [opinions]. But more than that was a freshness of his prose that reflected a clarity of thinking which commanded attention."

With the goal of communicating, like Holmes, in a way that "commands attention," take some time to play around with ways AI tools might help you "half-life your message." You can stick with the recording you already made. You don't need to make up new material. But you may have to experiment a bit, because this part of the exercise intentionally doesn't come with a long list of explicit steps. The reason: One of the main goals of this book is to give you the confidence and conceptual vocabulary to explore various AI tools on your own—and exploration often involves a fair amount of missteps and dead ends. I'd rather you discover, by yourself, a few techniques that don't work than simply follow, without thinking, the ones I think will work.

That said, I will provide a few examples from students of mine who have completed the exercise, in case they might help inform your own approach.

Student #1

I used Microsoft Word to transcribe my original 60-second recording. I then took that transcription and put it into ChatGPT, asking it to identify the key points of the speech. Next, I took those key points and reuploaded them in a new chat to ask it to make me 30-second and 15-second speeches. I found the half-lifeing by AI to be much stronger than what I did. It was able to distill and articulate my key points much faster than I would have in my rambles.

Student #2

After transcribing my original recordings, I took the 60-second recording and placed it into ChatGPT. I asked ChatGPT to cut the text in half. It did that quite successfully. In fact, this version was actually better than what I had originally stated in my 30-second version. It was clear, concise, and to the point.

I then asked ChatGPT to take the concise version and reduce that further. But that's where ChatGPT ran into problems. It simply rearranged the words and ended up creating a passage longer than the one I inputted.

Bottom line: If I had a really long passage I needed to cut, I would definitely use ChatGPT to assist; otherwise, I wouldn't use it.

Student #3

I used voice typing in Google Docs to transcribe my speech. I then asked ChatGPT to help shorten the text. It did a very good job and seemed to be better than the "half-lifeing" I did on my own. Trying to think out loud was difficult for me. Having AI helped me to be concise and create a better message.

Student #4

I asked the chatbot to "distill the following text into a more cogent message." It gave an okay result, but I wasn't really satisfied. I didn't feel like it really got to the core of what I wanted to say.

So I then told it that (1) I was looking to reduce the message by half and (2) it could bring in outside information so long as the information aligned with the text I had already provided. The response the chatbot gave was very solid, but it was still missing any direct mention of one of the key terms my original message included: "disparate impact." When, however, I told it that I really liked what it had come up with but that I wanted it to explicitly add a connection to "disparate impact," the output it generated was exactly what I wanted—pithy, with the important key points.

It feels embarrassing to say, but ultimately the chatbot version was enormously better than mine.

CHAPTER 25

Feedback vs. Advice

I generate a lot of writing both for my work and for my hobbies, and a lot of time I run out of people who are excited to give me first-pass edits.

—Charles Becker, "Ways People are Using AI" (2023)

We've been talking a lot about how to get AI feedback. But we should also talk about how to *process* AI feedback, because the right approach is certainly not immediate, uncritical acceptance.

Remember the critique we encountered in the "Title Search" exercise when we were learning about the book *AI Snake Oil* by two Princeton computer scientists. They're the ones who have called ChatGPT "the greatest bullshitter ever" and pointed out that "even though [ChatGPT] often gives excellent answers, sometimes it fails badly. And it's always convincing, so it's hard to tell the difference."

That's not really a great recipe for sound, evidence-based advice. I've never heard someone praise their favorite teacher, coach, counselor, or mentor by describing them as "the greatest bullshitter ever." There is a difference, however, between advice—which is designed to be followed—and feedback, which can be a more amorphous (and sometimes inconsistent) collection of reactions.

If you have ever had multiple people offer their opinion of a document you've written, a presentation you delivered, or even an outfit you decided to wear, you've probably experienced that inconsistency for yourself.

You've also probably been in a situation in which the feedback you received from somebody was completely off base and ill informed—but it nevertheless helped you see something about your writing, your thinking, or possibly your own behavior that you hadn't previously realized.

The solution the person proposes (the advice) may not be worth paying attention to. But their feedback is. Their comments may productively push you to consider a new perspective or simply cause you to spot a flaw you previously overlooked. Feedback doesn't have to be "right" to be valuable.

The psychologist Adam Grant, who is the author of *Think Again* and many other highly acclaimed books, captured this "feedback vs. advice" distinction when he interviewed the writer George Saunders back in 2023. "I've often found myself telling my students," Grant explained, "that the reason that other people can see problems you can't is you're too close to your own work, and they have distance. But that same distance makes them terrible at solving your problem because they often don't know what other problems they're creating."

Or consider the following observation by Haruki Murakami in *Novelist as a Vocation*, a book that chronicles Murakami's transformation from the owner of a small jazz bar in Tokyo to an international literary powerhouse whose work has received awards from prize panels in Ireland, Spain, Denmark, Germany, the Czech Republic, and many other countries, including his home nation of Japan: "It seems that when a reader has a problem [with a draft I've written], there is usually *something* that needs fixing, whether or not it corresponds to their suggestions. In short, the flow of their reading has been *blocked*. It is my job, then, to eliminate that blockage, to unclog the pipe, as it were."

The results of this process—where, regardless of whether Murakami implements or even agrees with somebody's recommended edits, he still uses their feedback as an opportunity to reflect on and tinker with his current approach—have been, according to him, consistently positive. "Whichever course I have followed, once I have sat down and rewritten a given section I almost always find it much improved."

The following are examples of people using AI feedback to experience a similar benefit, in a wide range of domains. With any luck, their feedback experiments will spark some ideas of your own.

Negotiation

One of my favorite examples is people using it to practice their negotiation skills. They can put the AI as an adversary. They can put the AI to argue better on their behalf. But they're not just using it as a fancy search engine. They're using it for role play.

—Oren Etzioni (professor emeritus of computer science at the University of Washington), "The AI Revolution: Myths, Risks, and Opportunities"

Public Speaking

According to the students, AI feedback led them to reflect on their performance and targets for development. Most students seemed satisfied with AI feedback because it felt neutral and unbiased and thus was easy to receive. Although AI feedback on single features was surprising to some, most students reported that the feedback met their expectations, which was thought to enhance the credibility of AI.

It was interesting to obtain the results from the machine because they did not involve any personal history or chemistry. The feedback from the machine was easy and neutral to receive. The numbers roused interest, and they gave new kinds of pointers on development areas.

Feedback from AI largely focused on paralinguistic features. Many students received feedback on speaking too fast or too slow. Some received feedback concerning the pitch of their voices, which evoked confusion. For example, one student wondered why AI provides feedback on pitch because it reinforces gender stereotypes. Additionally, some would have wanted more detailed information on the basis of AI feedback. The weak point was thought to be the AI's inability to consider the subject, context, or target audience of the speech.

—Pekka Isotalus, Marja Eklund, and Karoliina Karppinen, "Artificial Intelligence as a Feedback Provider in Practicing Public Speaking"

Interior Decorating

I use it for interior decorating—I'll upload a photo of a room in my house and say, "Give this room a glow-up. Tell me what furniture to buy and how to arrange it. [Then] generate the 'after' picture."

—Kevin Roose (tech columnist at *The New York Times*), "Everyone Is Using A.I. for Everything. Is That Bad?"

Exam Prep

I used ChatGPT to help me study for my Federal Courts final exam. I inputted my answers from a practice midterm I took earlier in the semester and asked for feedback. This was interesting because I was able to compare ChatGPT's feedback to the feedback from my professor. The feedback from ChatGPT was very similar to my professor's. I then went back and forth with ChatGPT, asking it to expand on the feedback it gave. I would recommend the prompts I used. I first asked it broadly for general feedback, then I homed in on specific things it said.

I wish I had thought of using ChatGPT this way in previous semesters. I think it would have been super helpful.

—Law student in one of my classes

CEO Coaching

I use [ChatGPT] to bounce ideas off of before I ask my team, in case it's an embarrassing question.

—Bridget McCormack (former Chief Justice of the Michigan Supreme Court and current CEO of the American Arbitration Association), "Generative AI in Legal Practice: Adapting to New Ethical Standards and Regulations"

CHAPTER 26

Work, Responsibility, and Play

I just want to say that history, when it arrives, may not look as you expect, based on the reading of history books. Things in there are always so clear.

—George Saunders, "Love Letter"

We've now reached the end of the book. At the very beginning of it, we talked about a phrase that seemed to capture the very common feeling of being overwhelmed and disoriented by recent advances in AI and the rapid pace of technological development in general. Borrowing from the journalists Alex Steffen and Ira Glass, we called the feeling being "unprepared for what has already happened."

My hope is that our time together has now made you at least a little *less* unprepared for what has already happened in the world of AI—and what may happen in the future:

- You now know, thanks to Part 1 ("Obstacles and Opportunities"), about developing mechanical sympathy, becoming conspicuously good, and avoiding "AI Snake Oil."
- You also know, thanks to Part 2 ("Communication and Creativity") and Part 3 ("Time and Tasks"), about the risks—and the rewards—of using AI to help with your writing skills, your speaking skills, your creativity, and your ability to both manage time and efficiently complete tasks. Digital delegation may become an increasingly important skill in the coming years, but we'll also always want to remember the emptiness and regret brought on by delegation remorse.
- Finally, thanks to Part 4 ("Learning and Leading"), you have gotten to see what some students, teachers, and leaders *love* about AI and what some students, teachers, and leaders *hate* about AI.

A good example of that educational tension comes from the campus of Emory University in Atlanta, Georgia. Here's how the key events were described in an article in *The Wall Street Journal*:

> College student Benjamin Craver was flying high. It was March 2023 and the artificial intelligence tool he helped launch won a $10,000 first-place prize at his university's startup competition.

Six months later, Emory University suspended him and his co-founder for that same AI tool.

The tool, called Eightball, was designed to help students study. "Users upload classroom slides or notes," the article explained, "and the tool uses that information to create flashcards and practice test questions." So you can see why it caught the attention—in a positive way—of the judges of the startup competition. "I for one wish that Eightball had been available when I was a student," one of them wrote in a letter of support Craver included in a lawsuit against the university. Craver was hoping to make Emory reverse its decision and wipe the suspension from his permanent record.

The honor council that issued the suspension, however, saw things much differently. It was concerned that the tool could be used for cheating and concluded it violated the school's policy against connecting an external program to the software platform that professors use to post homework assignments, class notes, and other course materials.

The lawsuit was eventually settled out of court, but I don't think it will be the last time we see a conflict between, on the one hand, AI innovation and, on the other, academic integrity. Software updates can happen in a matter of seconds. But institutional updates often take years or even decades, as do many individual human updates. "Our ethical evolution still lags behind our technological revolutions," Virginia Eubanks writes in the *Automating Inequality* book we talked about in Chapter 21 ("Producing More, Understanding Less").

Or think back to the epigraph that opened Chapter 2 ("Unprepared for What Has Already Happened"). I took it from an autobiography first published in 1907 by Henry Adams, who was the direct descendant of

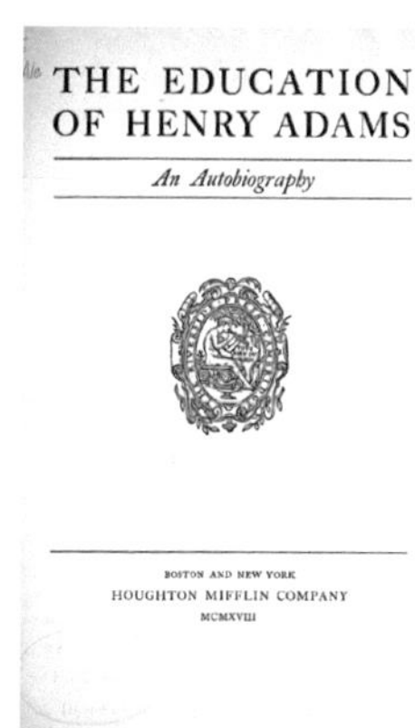
THE EDUCATION OF HENRY ADAMS

An Autobiography

BOSTON AND NEW YORK
HOUGHTON MIFFLIN COMPANY
MCMXVIII

two American presidents: John Quincy Adams (Henry's grandfather) and John Adams (Henry's great-grandfather). The quote, which I am about to share again, describes the existential whiplash Adams experienced at the beginning of the 20th century, when a different set of technological revolutions was taking place. At once impressed and terrified by all the new machines and inventions on display at the 1900 World's Fair in Paris, Adams wrote that, as he walked through the exhibition, he felt as if he had "his historical neck broken by the sudden eruption of forces totally new."

Fortunately, Adams soon found comfort in realizing that other generations had gone through something similar without the world coming to an end. "The year 1900 was not the first to upset schoolmasters," he reminds us. "Copernicus and Galileo had broken many professorial necks around 1600," and "Columbus had stood the world on its head towards 1500." He even sees parallels as far back as the year 310, "when Constantine set up the Cross."

I find a lot of comfort in that kind of long-term perspective, which is why I'd like to close the book with the thoughts of someone who often thought in terms of not just years but decades, centuries, and

even millennia. He is also the person who actually coined, in 1959, the term "knowledge worker": the legendary business professor Peter Drucker, for whom the Peter F. Drucker School of Management at Claremont University is named.

"Tremendous though today's technological explosion is," Drucker wrote in a 1966 essay called "The First Technological Revolution and Its Lessons," just as the modern computer age was starting to take shape, "it is hardly greater than the first great revolution technology wrought in human life." Skeptical of "those among us who predict a technological heaven and those who predict a technological hell of 'alienation,' of 'technological unemployment,'" he instead offers a no-nonsense approach to navigating extreme change: "A time of true technological revolution is not a time for exultation. It is not a time for despair either. It is a time for work and responsibility."

I'll add that I think it is also a time for something else: play.

One of the courses on artificial intelligence I teach is called "AI Sandbox" because I want to communicate to everyone who takes it that there are significant benefits to adopting an exploratory mindset when interacting with new tools and ideas. We make plenty of room in the "sandbox" for rigor, analysis, and critique. But we also put a premium on wonder, discovery, improvisation, and just plain fun.

My hope is that, long after you finish this book, you take a similarly expansive, multidimensional approach to engaging with AI. If you do, I'm confident that you'll discover some extremely useful AI tips of your own while simultaneously avoiding the most pernicious AI traps.

PHOTO CREDITS

Chapter 1

"Felix Frankfurter." July 12, 1918. Harris and Ewing Collection, PPOC, Library of Congress, Reproduction Number: LC-USZ62-36966. https://www.loc.gov/pictures/item/2004671904/

Peabody Awards. "Ira Glass at the 73rd Annual Peabody Awards ii (cropped)." Licensed under CC BY 2.0. https://commons.wikimedia.org/wiki/File:Ira_Glass_at_the_73rd_Annual_Peabody_Awards_ii_(cropped).jpg

Chapter 2

Christopher Wilson. "Mustafa Suleyman photo (cropped)." Licensed under CC BY-SA 4.0. https://en.wikipedia.org/wiki/Mustafa_Suleyman#/media/File:Mustafa_Suleyman_photo.jpg

Chapter 3

espinya. "Matra MS10—Jackie Stewart—panoramio." Licensed under CC BY-SA 3.0. https://commons.wikimedia.org/wiki/File:Matra_MS10_-_Jackie_Stewart_-_panoramio.jpg

Hossein Zohrevand. "Lionel-Messi-Argentina-2022-FIFA-World-Cup sharpness." Licensed under CC BY 4.0. https://commons

.wikimedia.org/wiki/File:Lionel-Messi-Argentina-2022-FIFA-World-Cup_sharpness.jpg

Amerpear. "Marta Brazil" Licensed under CC BY-SA 4.0. https://commons.wikimedia.org/wiki/File:Marta_Brazil.jpg

"17th-Century Sports Car Image" generated with DALL-E AI Art Generator, modern sports car in a field surrounded by 17th-century townspeople (2025).

AI Exercise #1: Title Search

Laubenstein Ronald. "Girl Stands on Shore and Fishes with Her Fishing Rod." Available in the public domain. https://en.wikipedia.org/wiki/File:Girl_stands_on_shore_and_fishes_with_her_fishing_rod.jpg

Frankie Fouganthin. "Teatersport." January 2013. Licensed under CC BY-SA 3.0. https://commons.wikimedia.org/wiki/File:Teatersport_-4.jpg

AI Exercise #2: Picture This

Eric Chan. "Witness impeachment." Licensed under CC BY 2.0. https://en.wikipedia.org/wiki/Mock_trial#/media/File:Witness_impeachment.jpg

Chuck Kennedy (US Department of State). "Photograph of Secretary Antony Blinken signing the 123 Agreement for trade between the United States and the Philippines." November 2023. Wikimedia Commons. https://commons.wikimedia.org/wiki/File:Secretary_Blinken_Attends_the_Philippines_123_Agreement_Signing_Ceremony_%2853337923885%29.jpg

Sarah Mirk. "Photograph of Molly Crabapple at the 2011 Stumptown Comics Fest." April 2011. Wikimedia Commons. https://commons.wikimedia.org/wiki/File:Molly_Crabapple_at_Stumptown_Comics_Fest_2011.jpg

Jay Adams. "Stephanie Dinkins." https://news.stonybrook.edu/facultystaff/stephanie-dinkins-named-inaugural-yayoi-kusama-endowed-professor-of-art/

Chapter 11

Jacques-Louis David. "The Death of Socrates (1787) (cropped)." Wikimedia Commons. https://commons.wikimedia.org/wiki/File:The_Death_of_Socrates_cropped.jpg

AI Exercise #4: The Language of Common Life

"Portrait of Charles G. Finney (19th Century)." Wikimedia Commons. https://commons.wikimedia.org/wiki/File:Charles_g_finney.jpg

Alexander Gardner. "Photograph of Abraham Lincoln." November 8, 1863. Wikimedia Commons. https://commons.wikimedia.org/wiki/File:Abraham_Lincoln_1863_Portrait_(3x4_cropped).jpg

Cecile van Straten. "Photograph of Nigella Lawson giving an interview in Manilla, Philippines (Sept. 6, 2016) (cropped)." Wikimedia Commons. https://commons.wikimedia.org/wiki/File:Nigella_Lawson_in_Manilla_-_2017_%2829946044613%29_%28cropped%29.jpg

"Photograph of Anthony Bourdain." May 23, 2014. Wikimedia Commons. https://commons.wikimedia.org/wiki/File:Anthony_Bourdain_Peabody_2014b.jpg

Chapter 15

Futuristic Conference. Image generated with Adobe Firefly AI Art Generator, futuristic business meeting (2025).

"Photograph of the United States Supreme Court Building." March 12, 2019. Wikimedia Commons. Licensed for distribution under the

Creative Commons Attribution-Share Alike 4.0 International license. https://commons.wikimedia.org/wiki/File:Supreme_Court_of_the_U.S._Building.jpg

Steve Petteway. "Official Portrait of Justice Sonia Sotomayor." August 21, 2009. Wikimedia Commons. https://en.wikipedia.org/wiki/File:Sonia_Sotomayor_in_SCOTUS_robe.jpg

Chapter 16

Pink Sherbert Photography, *Blank Pages in an Open Notebook*, 2010, photograph. Wikimedia Commons, https://commons.wikimedia.org/wiki/File:Blank_Pages_In_An_Open_Notebook_(4812269151).jpg. Licensed under [CC BY 2.0 / CC BY-SA 2.0].

OJjnr, *Bridal Shower*, photograph. Wikimedia Commons, https://commons.wikimedia.org/wiki/File:Bridal_Shower_1_76.jpg. Licensed under CC BY-SA 4.0.

Chapter 23

Department for Education logo. © Crown copyright. Reproduced under fair use for purposes of identification and critical commentary.

Chapter 24

ITU Pictures. *Rumman Chowdhury at the AI for Good Global Summit 2018*, photograph. Wikimedia Commons, https://commons.wikimedia.org/wiki/File:Rumman_Chowdhury_at_the_AI_for_Good_Global_Summit_2018_(42110666692).jpg. Licensed under CC BY 2.0.

JoeyBLS. "Hobart Welcome Sign: Hobart, Indiana." Public Domain. https://en.wikipedia.org/wiki/File:HobartIN.jpg

AI Exercise #6: Half-Life Your Message

Pearson Scott Foresman. "*Guillotine (PSF)*, digital line drawing." Available in the public domain. https://commons.wikimedia.org/wiki/File:Guillotine_(PSF).png

Harris & Ewing. "Oliver Wendell Holmes, Jr. circa 1930-Edit." Licensed under CC BY-SA. https://commons.wikimedia.org/wiki/File:Oliver_Wendell_Holmes_Jr_circa_1930-edit.jpg

Chapter 25

Haruki Murakami. "Photo Signed by Haruki Murakami." Society for Culture, Art, and International Cooperation Adigat. Licensed under CC 4.0. https://commons.wikimedia.org/wiki/File:Photo_signed_by_Haruki_Murakami.jpg

Chapter 26

"Title page of *The Education of Henry Adams* by Henry Adams (1918)." Available in the public domain. https://commons.wikimedia.org/wiki/File:The_Education_of_Henry_Adams_(1918)_title_page.jpg

George Peter Alexander Healy. "John Quincy Adams." 1858. Available in the public domain. https://commons.wikimedia.org/wiki/File:John_Quincy_Adams_by_GPA_Healy,_1858.jpg

Gilbert Stuart. "John Adams." Available in the public domain. https://commons.wikimedia.org/wiki/File:John_Adams_A18236.jpg

Jeff McNeil, "Peter F. Drucker sitting in a library." Licensed under CC BY-SA. https://commons.wikimedia.org/wiki/File:Drucker5789.jpg

Artaxerxes. "Child Play in Our Community Place Sandbox at the Lawn Jam June 28, 2008 in Harrisonburg, Virginia" 2008. Licensed under CC BY-SA 3.0. https://commons.wikimedia.org/wiki/File:Sandbox_Lawn_Jam_Our_Community_Place_Harrisonburg_VA_June_2008.jpg

NOTES

Chapter 1

4 **"conspicuously good":** Brad Snyder, *Democratic Justice* (New York: W. W. Norton, 2022), 27.

5 **"one every two to three hours":** "What Are the Risks of Generative AI? The Turing Lectures with Mhairi Aitken," Royal Institution, YouTube, November 9, 2023, 1:01:29, https://www.youtube.com/watch?v=si1jcl7UFqU.

5 **"bogus, overhyped AI products":** Arvind Narayanan and Sayash Kapoor, *AI Snake Oil* (Princeton: Princeton University Press, 2024).

6 **"unprepared for what has already happened":** "Unprepared for What Has Already Happened," *This American Life* podcast, produced by WBEZ Chicago, March 15, 2024, 6:39, https://www.thisamericanlife.org/826/unprepared-for-what-has-already-happened.

Chapter 2

8 **"the unsettling feeling":** Elizabeth Weil, "This Isn't the California I Married," *New York Times Magazine*, January 3, 2022, https://www.nytimes.com/2022/01/03/magazine/california-widfires.html.

8 **"My fifty-two-year-old body":** Cade Metz, *Genius Makers: The Mavericks Who Brought AI to Google, Facebook, and the World* (New York: Dutton, 2022), 56.

8 **"MIT physicist Max Tegmark":** Max Tegmark, *Life 3.0: Being Human in the Age of Artificial Intelligence* (New York: Knopf, 2017), 86.

8 **"more AI-related products":** Nick Bilton, "Artificial Intelligence May Be Humanity's Most Ingenious Invention—and Its Last?," *Vanity Fair*, September 13, 2023, https://www.vanityfair.com/news/2023/09/artificial-intelligence-industry-future.

9 **"like a part of my identity":** "Anthropic's C.E.O., Dario Amodei, on Surviving the A.I. Endgame," *Hard Fork* podcast, produced by *The New York Times*, February 28, 2025, 42:20, https://www.nytimes.com/2025/02/28/podcasts/hardfork-anthropic-dario-amodei.html?showTranscript=1.

9 **"Even as the one who's building these":** Ibid., 42:39.

9 **"First come more efficient ways":** Mustafa Suleyman with Michael Bhaskar, *The Coming Wave: Technology, Power, and the Twenty-First Century's Greatest Dilemma* (New York: Crown, 2023), 12.

9 **"the coming wave":** Ibid., 178.

10 **"We have enormous control":** Joe Weisenthal and Tracy Alloway, "The Economist Who Believes AI Will Be Great for the Middle Class," *Odd Lots with Joe Weisenthal and Tracy Alloway* podcast, March 22, 2024, 35:20, https://www.bloomberg.com/news/audio/2024-03-22/odd-lots-will-ai-be-great-for-the-middle-class-podcast.

10 **"first scientific paper on neural networks":** Warren S. McCulloch and Walter Pitts, "A Logical Calculus of the Ideas Immanent in Nervous Activity," *Bulletin of Mathematical Biophysics* 5, no. 1 (1943): 115.

Chapter 3

12 **"how a machine will respond":** "Martin Thompson on Mechanical Sympathy," *Software Engineering Radio* podcast, February 19, 2014, https://www.se-radio.net/2014/02/episode-201-martin-thompson-on-mechanical-sympathy/.

12 **"sense for the machine's strengths":** James Somers, "A Coder Considers the Waning Days of the Craft," *The New Yorker*, November 13, 2023, https://www.newyorker.com/magazine/2023/11/20/a-coder-considers-the-waning-days-of-the-craft.

12 **"You don't need to be an engineer":** Andrei Chichak, "On Mechanical Sympathy," *Embedded.fm*, April 20, 2016, https://embedded.fm/blog/2016/4/18/on-mechanincal-sympathy; Somers, "Coder Considers."

13 **"made this point well":** "Making Magic with Gen AI: Capital One's Prem Natarajan," *Me, Myself, and AI* podcast, produced by *MIT Sloan Management Review*, January 3, 2024, https://sloanreview.mit.edu/audio/making-magic-with-gen-ai-capital-ones-prem-natarajan/.

14 **"need to be careful and deliberate":** Ibid., 19:25.

14 **"think through the implications":** Ibid.

14 **"like we're in the 17th century":** "Superintelligent AI—the Utopians," *Tech Tonic* podcast, produced by the *Financial Times*, November 21, 2023, https://www.ft.com/content/dd762da9-5d41-4462-aafa-6de5b511405c.

14 **"The problem with AI":** *Last Week Tonight with John Oliver: Artificial Intelligence*, directed by Paul Pennolino, broadcast February 26, 2023, HBO.

16 **"concerned with truth":** Michael Townsen Hicks et al., "ChatGPT Is Bullshit," *Ethics and Information Technology*, June 8, 2024, 38.

16 **"without regard for the truth":** Arvind Narayanan and Sayash Kapoor, "ChatGPT Is a Bullshit Generator. But It Can Still Be Amazingly Useful," AI as Normal Technology, December 6, 2022, https://www.aisnakeoil.com/p/chatgpt-is-a-bullshit-generator-but.

16 **"often gives excellent answers":** Ibid.

Chapter 4

22 **"weird, somewhat alien interns":** Ethan Mollick, *Co-Intelligence: Living and Working with AI* (New York: Portfolio, 2024).

22 **"sometimes lie":** Ibid.

23 **"unsettlingly error-prone":** William H. Walters and Esther Isabelle Wilder, "Fabrication and Errors in the Bibliographic Citations Generated by ChatGPT," *Scientific Reports*, September 7, 2023, article 14045; Varun Magesh et al., "Hallucination-Free? Assessing the Reliability of Leading AI Legal Research Tools," *Journal of Empirical Legal Studies* 22 (2025): 216.

23 **"fabricate news stories":** Emily Olson, "Google Shares Drop $100 Billion After Its New AI Chatbot Makes a Mistake," NPR, February 9, 2023, https://www.npr.org/2023/02/09/1155650909/google-chatbot--error-bard-shares.

23 **"The incident highlighted issues":** *Arve Hjalmar Holmen v. OpenAI OpCo, LLC*, No. C096, Complaint ¶ 5 (Datatilsynet [Norwegian Data

Protection Authority], 2025), https://noyb.eu/sites/default/files/2025-03/OpenAI_complaint_redacted.pdf.

23 **"a claim of sexual harassment":** Jonathan Turley, "Defamed by ChatGPT: My Own Bizarre Experience with Artificiality of 'Artificial Intelligence,'" JonathanTurley.org, April 6, 2023, https://jonathanturley.org/2023/04/06/defamed-by-chatgpt-my-own-bizarre-experience-with-artificiality-of-artificial-intelligence/.

24 **"article that didn't actually exist":** Pranshu Verma and Will Oremus, "Chat GPT Invented a Sexual Harassment Scandal and Named a Real Law Prof as the Accused," *Washington Post*, April 5, 2023, https://www.washingtonpost.com/technology/2023/04/05/chatgpt-lies/.

24 **"In the meantime":** Turley, "Defamed by ChatGPT."

24 **"It's one thing":** Tom Gerken, "ChatGPT: Mayor Starts Legal Bid over False Bribery Claim," BBC News, April 6, 2023, https://www.bbc.com/news/technology-65202597.

24 **"played a key role":** David Swan, "Australian Mayor Abandons World-First ChatGPT Lawsuit," *Sydney Morning Herald*, February 12, 2024, https://www.smh.com.au/technology/australian-mayor-abandons-world-first-chatgpt-lawsuit-20240209-p5f3nf.html.

25 **"hallucinations persist":** Magesh et al., "Hallucination-Free?"

25 **"One study, for example":** Matthew Dahl et al., "Large Legal Fictions: Profiling Legal Hallucinations in Large Language Models," *Journal of Legal Analysis* 16 (2024): 64.

25 **"A follow-up project":** Magesh et al., "Hallucination-Free?"

25 **"the hallucination rate":** Serena Wellen, "How Lexis+ AI Delivers Hallucination-Free Linked Legal Citations," *LexisNexis: Legal Insights*, May 2, 2024, https://www.lexisnexis.com/community/insights/legal/b/product-features/posts/how-lexis-ai-delivers-hallucination-free-linked-legal-citations; Casetext, "GPT-4 Alone Is Not a Reliable Legal Solution—but It Does Enable One: Cocounsel Harnesses GPT-4's Power to Deliver Results That Legal Professionals Can Rely On," Thomson Reuters, May 5, 2023, https://web.archive.org/web/20241219202017/https://casetext.com/blog/cocounsel-harnesses-gpt-4s-power-to-deliver-results-that-legal-professionals-can-rely-on/.

25 **"those kinds of error rates":** Arvind Narayanan and Sayash Kapoor, "ChatGPT Is a Bullshit Generator. But It Can Still Be Amazingly Useful," AI as Normal Technology, December 6, 2022, https://www.aisnakeoil.com/p/chatgpt-is-a-bullshit-generator-but.

25 **"true statements as a side effect":** Ibid.

25 **"Humans, of course":** For interesting accounts of individual bullshitters, see Frank W. Abagnale, *Catch Me If You Can* (Edinburgh: Mainstream, 2003); Rachel DeLoache Williams, *My Friend Anna* (New York: Gallery Books, 2019); Diana B. Henriques, *The Wizard of Lies* (New York: St. Martin's Griffin, 2011); David Maurer, *The Big Con* (New York: Anchor Books, 1999); and Tori Telfer, *Confident Women* (New York: Harper Perennial, 2021).

26 **"blatantly make false statements":** "Artificial Intelligence, Defamation, and New Speech Frontiers," *We the People* podcast, produced by the National Constitution Center, June 8, 2023, 15:13, https://constitutioncenter.org/news-debate/podcasts/artificial-intelligence-defamation-and-new-speech-frontiers.

26 **"history of humankind":** Juan Jacinto Muñoz-Rengel, *A History of Lying* (Cambridge: Polity, 2022), 1; see also Jeremy Campbell, *The Liar's Tale: A History of Falsehood* (New York: W. W. Norton, 2002).

26 **"rapid technological change":** Kevin Roose, *Futureproof: 9 Rules for Surviving in the Age of AI* (New York: Random House, 2022).

26 **"optimal level of hallucination":** "Mayhem at OpenAI + Our Interview with Sam Altman," *Hard Fork* podcast, produced by *The New York Times*, November 20, 2023, 51:10, https://www.nytimes.com/2023/11/20/podcasts/mayhem-at-openai-our-interview-with-sam-altman.html?showTranscript=1.

26 **"Altman agreed":** Ibid., 52:05.

26 **"You want it to be reliable":** Ibid., 51:30.

27 **"controllability":** Ibid.

32 **"I truly don't understand":** "Why AI Is a Threat to Artists," *Tech Won't Save Us* podcast, June 29, 2023, 9:00, https://www.techwontsave.us/episode/174_why_ai_is_a_threat_to_artists_w_molly_crabapple.

32 **"most influential people in AI":** "Time100 AI," *Time*, September 7, 2023, https://time.com/collection/time100-ai/.

32 **"What is this technology doing":** Zachary Small, "Black Artists Say A.I. Shows Bias, with Algorithms Erasing Their History," *The New York Times*, July 4, 2023, https://www.nytimes.com/2023/07/04/arts/design/black-artists-bias-ai.html.

33 **"Art is the aftershock":** Steven Johnson, *Wonderland: How Play Made the Modern World* (New York: Riverhead Books, 2016), 175.

33 **"Sometimes the aftershock":** Ibid.

Chapter 5

36 **"Think of those lawyers":** Erin Mulvaney, "Judge Sanctions Lawyers Who Filed Fake ChatGPT Legal Research," *Wall Street Journal*, June 22, 2023, https://www.wsj.com/articles/judge-sanctions-lawyers-who-filed-fake-chatgpt-legal-research-9ebad8f9.

37 **"firms that effectively leverage":** John Villasenor, "How AI Will Revolutionize the Practice of Law," Brookings, March 20, 2023, https://www.brookings.edu/articles/how-ai-will-revolutionize-the-practice-of-law/.

37 **"Villasenor's essay":** Ibid.

37 **"endangered occupational species":** Steve Lohr, "A.I. Is Coming for Lawyers, Again," *The New York Times*, April 10, 2023, https://www.nytimes.com/2023/04/10/technology/ai-is-coming-for-lawyers-again.html.

37 **"number of lawyers in the United States":** American Bar Association, *National Lawyer Population Survey: Lawyer Population by State, 2022*, https://www.americanbar.org/content/dam/aba/administrative/market_research/2022-national-lawyer-population-survey.pdf.

37 **"time had come to reevaluate":** Fei-Fei Li, *The Worlds I See: Curiosity, Exploration, and Discovery at the Dawn of AI* (New York: Flatiron, 2025) 300.

Chapter 6

42 **"When is the last time":** Todd Rogers and Jessica Lasky-Fink, *Writing for Busy Readers* (New York: Dutton, 2023).

42 **"I hardly have time":** "Microsoft's AI Perspective: From Chatbots to Reengineering the Organization," *Managing the Future of Work* podcast, produced by Harvard Business School, February 21, 2024, https://www

.hbs.edu/managing-the-future-of-work/podcast/Pages/podcast-details .aspx?episode=1617731410.

42 **"average time taken":** Shakked Noy and Whitney Zhang, "Experimental Evidence on the Productivity Effects of Generative Artificial Intelligence," working paper, MIT Department of Economics, March 6, 2023, https://papers.ssrn.com/sol3/papers.cfm?abstract_id=4375283.

42 **"experiment involving law students":** Jonathan H. Choi, Amy B. Monahan, and Daniel Schwarcz, "Lawyering in the Age of Artificial Intelligence," *Minnesota Law Review* 109 (2024): 147; Fabrizio Dell'Acqua et al., "Navigating the Jagged Technological Frontier: Field Experimental Evidence of the Effects of AI on Knowledge Worker Productivity and Quality," Harvard Business School Working Paper No. 24-013, 2023.

43 **"AI assistance was particularly beneficial":** Erik Brynjolfsson et al., "Generative AI at Work," National Bureau of Economic Research Working Paper No. 31161, 2023.

43 **"Without access to an AI tool":** Brian Eastwood, "Workers with Less Experience Gain the Most from Generative AI," MIT Sloan, June 26, 2023, https://mitsloan.mit.edu/ideas-made-to-matter/workers-less -experience-gain-most-generative-ai.

43 **"The reality is":** Julia Angwin, "Press Pause on the Silicon Valley Hype Machine," *The New York Times*, May 15, 2024, https://www.nytimes .com/2024/05/15/opinion/artificial-intelligence-ai-openai-chatgpt -overrated-hype.html.

43 **"One way I think":** "Will A.I. Break the Internet? Or Save It?," *The Ezra Klein Show* podcast, produced by *The New York Times*, April 5, 2024, 1:01:50, https://www.nytimes.com/2024/04/05/opinion/ezra-klein -podcast-nilay-patel.html.

43 **"don't have interns write":** Ibid.

44 **"produce more but understand less":** Lisa Messeri and M. J. Crockett, "Artificial Intelligence and Illusions of Understanding in Scientific Research," *Nature* 627 (2024): 49.

Chapter 7

46 **"the greatest skill":** "The AI Revolution Could Be Bigger and Weirder Than We Can Imagine," *Plain English* podcast, March 21, 2023, https://

www.theringer.com/2023/03/21/tech/the-ai-revolution-could-be-bigger-and-weirder-than-we-can-imagine.

46 **"I really believe":** Ilona Logvinova, "What Every Managing Partner & C-Suite Leader Needs to Know About Legal AI," panel discussion, January 31, 2024, hosted by the *Wall Street Journal* at the Harvard Club in New York City, https://wsjcustomevents.com/lexisnexis2024.

46 **"hide from the blank page":** "Will AI Replace Me?," *Fixable* podcast, produced by TED, October 16, 2023, 1:18, https://www.ted.com/podcasts/fixable/will-ai-replace-me-w-aj-jacobs-transcript.

46 **"endowed progress effect":** Joseph C. Nunes and Xavier Drèze, "The Endowed Progress Effect: How Artificial Advancement Increases Effort," *Journal of Consumer Research* 32 (2006): 504.

47 **"more than twice as many people":** Dylan Lyons, "How Many People Speak English, and Where Is It Spoken?," Babbel, March 10, 2021, https://www.babbel.com/en/magazine/how-many-people-speak-english-and-where-is-it-spoken; "What Are the Top 200 Most Spoken Languages?," Ethnologue, 2025, https://www.ethnologue.com/insights/ethnologue200/.

47 **"global 'lingua franca'":** Sung Il Wang et al., "Is ChatGPT a 'Fire of Prometheus' for Non-Native English-Speaking Researchers in Academic Writing?," *Korean Journal of Radiology* 24 (2023): 952.

48 **"level the global playing field":** "Can AI Take a Joke?," *Freakonomics Radio* podcast, produced by Freakonomics, August 23, 2023, 35:07, https://freakonomics.com/podcast/can-a-i-take-a-joke/.

48 **"new modes of expression":** Ethan Mollick, *Co-Intelligence: Living and Working with AI* (New York: Portfolio, 2024), 32.

48 **"Since requiring AI":** Ibid.

48 **"clean, well-punctuated sentences":** "Generative AI Trends for 2024 with Tom Davenport," *Me, Myself, and AI* podcast, produced by *MIT Sloan Management Review*, February 6, 2024, 22:40, https://sloanreview.mit.edu/audio/bonus-episode-generative-ai-trends-for-2024-with-tom-davenport/.

Chapter 8

52 **"drafted by a chatbot":** Alexandra E. Petri, "After Michigan Shooting, One University Used ChatGPT to Offer Help to Students. It Backfired," *Los Angeles Times*, February 22, 2023, https://www.latimes.com/world-nation/story/2023-02-22/vanderbilt-university-apologizes-chatgpt-email-michigan-state-shooting; Megan Cerullo, "Vanderbilt Apologizes for ChatGPT-Generated Letter on Michigan State Shooting," CBS News, February 21, 2023, https://www.cbsnews.com/news/vanderbilt-apology-chatgpt-generated-message-msu-shooting/; Jennifer Korn, "Vanderbilt University Apologizes for Using ChatGPT to Write Mass-Shooting Email," CNN, February 22, 2023, https://www.cnn.com/2023/02/22/tech/vanderbilt-chatgpt-shooting-email/index.html.

52 **"sick and twisted irony":** Rachael Perrotta, "Peabody EDI Office Responds to MSU Shooting with Email Written Using ChatGPT," *Vanderbilt Hustler*, February 17, 2023, https://vanderbilthustler.com/2023/02/17/peabody-edi-office-responds-to-msu-shooting-with-email-written-using-chatgpt/.

53 **"hard to take a message seriously":** Ibid.

53 **"step back":** Aaditi Lele and Duaa Faquih, "Peabody EDI Deans Nicole Joseph, Hasina Mohyuddin Reinstated After Utilizing ChatGPT in Email About MSU Shooting," *Vanderbilt Hustler*, April 12, 2023, https://vanderbilthustler.com/2023/04/12/peabody-edi-deans-nicole-joseph-hasina-mohyuddin-reinstated-after-utilizing-chatgpt-to-write-an-email-about-msu-shooting/.

53 **"He toiled for hours":** Pranshu Verma and Will Oremus, "These Lawyers Used ChatGPT to Save Time. They Got Fired and Fined," *Washington Post*, November 16, 2023, https://www.washingtonpost.com/technology/2023/11/16/chatgpt-lawyer-fired-ai/.

53 **"chatbot had completed the document":** Ibid.

53 **"Before a hearing":** *People v. Crabill*, No. 23PDJ067, 2023 WL 8111898 (Colo. O.P.D.J. Nov. 22, 2023), https://www.coloradolegalregulation.com/wp-content/uploads/PDJ/Decisions/Crabill,%20Stipulation%20to%20Discipline,%2023PDJ067,%2011-22-23.pdf.

Chapter 9

55 **"Every decision we make":** Brian Christian, *The Alignment Problem: Machine Learning and Human Values* (New York: W. W. Norton, 2020), 131.

56 **"it would be naive":** Ethan Mollick, *Co-Intelligence: Living and Working with AI* (New York: Portfolio, 2024), 118–19.

56 **"explore different perspectives":** Ibid.

57 **"We rely on the machine":** Ibid.

57 **"a substitute for human effort":** Ibid., 120.

57 **"paste in the exact question":** Ibid., 120.

Chapter 10

60 **"intellectual autopilot":** Fabrizio Dell'Acqua, "Falling Asleep at the Wheel: Human/AI Collaboration in a Field Experiment on HR Recruiters," working paper, Laboratory for Innovation Science, Harvard Business School, https://www.dropbox.com/scl/fi/c5jdi146erky69csa8gha/Falling_Asleep_at_the_Wheel.pdf?rlkey=ss4vh6bsgzf52xiba8ffx0onc&e=1&st=s0ppis9g&dl=0.

60 **"human/AI collaboration":** Ibid., 1.

60 **"became more reliant on AI":** Ibid., 30.

61 **"maximizing the performance":** Ibid.

61 **"AI determinism":** Ibid.

61 **"human collaborators":** Ibid., 29.

Chapter 11

65 **"we're doing the hard thing":** "Will A.I. Break the Internet? Or Save It?," *The Ezra Klein Show* podcast, produced by *The New York Times*, April 5, 2024, 1:01:50, https://www.nytimes.com/2024/04/05/opinion/ezra-klein-podcast-nilay-patel.html.

65 **"give the A.I. a series of personal documents":** "How Should I Be Using A.I. Right Now?," *The Ezra Klein Show* podcast, produced by *The New York Times*, April 2, 2024, 24:24, https://www.nytimes.com/2024/04/02/opinion/ezra-klein-podcast-ethan-mollick.html.

66 **"moment of true metaphysical shock":** Ibid.

66 **“able to identify the tone”:** “Is A.I. Already Taking Jobs? + A Filmmaker Tries Sora + The XZ Backdoor Caper,” *Hard Fork* podcast, produced by *The New York Times*, April 5, 2024, 19:47, https://www.nytimes.com/2024/04/05/podcasts/hardfork-ai-jobs-sora-xz.html.

Chapter 12

68 **“customize your writing”:** Donald C. Bryant, “Rhetoric: Its Function and Its Scope,” *Quarterly Journal of Speech* 39, no. 4 (December 1953): 401.

68 **“many different social selves”:** William James, *The Principles of Psychology*, vol. 1, 1st ed. (New York: Henry Holt, 1890), 294, https://www.gutenberg.org/files/57628/57628-h/57628-h.htm.

69 **“‘high-context’ cultures”:** Erin Meyer, *The Culture Map: Breaking Through the Invisible Boundaries of Global Business* (New York: PublicAffairs, 2014), 29–60.

70 **“seek legitimate feedback”:** “AI for Self-Help and Legal Aid,” *Talk Justice: An LSC Podcast*, YouTube, July 30, 2024, https://www.youtube.com/watch?v=fIroeCMpYKA.

71 **“language of common life”:** Patrick Barry, *Good with Words: Speaking and Presenting* (Ann Arbor: Maize Books, 2021), 102–5.

71 **“preacher Charles Grandison Finney”:** Frances FitzGerald, *The Evangelicals: The Struggle to Shape America* (New York: Simon & Schuster, 2017).

71 **“looked at people in the audience”:** Ibid.

72 **“break down the most complex case”:** Doris Kearns Goodwin, *Leadership in Turbulent Times* (New York: Simon & Schuster, 2018).

74 **“erudite to brilliantly slangy”:** Patrick Radden Keefe, “Anthony Bourdain’s Moveable Feast,” *The New Yorker*, February 5, 2017, https://www.newyorker.com/magazine/2017/02/13/anthony-bourdains-moveable-feast.

75 **“talk to lay judges”:** *Proof in Trial with Cate Stetson* podcast, produced by Hogan Lovells, 2021, https://www.hoganlovells.com/en/publications/proof-in-trial-podcast-series.

76 **“conversations that we dread”:** Jeremy Utley and Kian Gohar, “For Conversations You Dread, Try a Chatbot,” *Wall Street Journal*, May 4,

2024, https://www.wsj.com/tech/ai/for-conversations-you-dread-try-a-chatbot-8eecb643.

Chapter 13

80 **"Many people worry":** Jeremy Utley and Kian Gohar, "For Conversations You Dread, Try a Chatbot," *Wall Street Journal*, May 4, 2024, https://www.wsj.com/tech/ai/for-conversations-you-dread-try-a-chatbot-8eecb643.

80 **"He had the AI role-play":** Ibid.

81 **"plausible next tokens":** Hannah Fry and Jeff Dean, "Decoding Google Gemini with Jeff Dean," *DeepMind Podcast*, YouTube, October 2024, https://www.youtube.com/watch?v=lH74gNeryhQ.

82 **"what other people miss":** Laila Lalami, *The Other Americans* (New York: Pantheon, 2019).

Chapter 14

86 **"space for the real healing":** Eric Topol, *Deep Medicine: How Artificial Intelligence Can Make Healthcare Human Again* (New York: Basic Books, 2019).

86 **"an A.I. helper":** Steve Lohr, "A.I. May Someday Work Medical Miracles. For Now, It Helps Do Paperwork," *The New York Times*, June 26, 2023, https://www.nytimes.com/2023/06/26/technology/ai-health-care-documentation.html.

86 **"freed up nearly two hours":** Ibid.

87 **"really a no-brainer":** Carolyn Elefant, "Can Lawyers Legally and Ethically Record Conversations with Clients Using Artificial Intelligence?," My Shingle, July 27, 2023, https://myshingle.com/2023/07/articles/artificial-intelligence/can-lawyers-legally-and-ethically-record-conversations-with-clients-using-artificial-intelligence/.

87 **"distraction of taking notes":** Ibid.

87 **"AI-transcripts":** Ibid.

87 **"ABA Formal Opinion 01-422":** John Bliss, "The Legal Ethics of Secret Client Recordings," *Georgetown Journal of Legal Ethics* 33 (2020): 55.

88 **"Copilot-generated summary":** Tom Dotan, "Early Adopters of Microsoft's AI Bot Wonder If It's Worth the Money," *Wall Street Journal*,

updated February 13, 2024, https://www.wsj.com/tech/ai/early-adopters-of-microsofts-ai-bot-wonder-if-its-worth-the-money-2e74e3a2.

88 **"become reliant on Copilot":** Ibid.

88 **"I'm going to skip this one":** Ibid.

Chapter 15

90 **"sensitive topics":** Brian X. Chen, "How to Use A.I. to Automate the Dreaded Office Meeting," *The New York Times*, June 9, 2023, https://www.nytimes.com/2023/06/09/technology/ai-meeting-assistant.html.

90 **"My friends coined a word":** "From the Toxic Culture That Gave Us Mansplaining and Manterrupting, Here Comes . . . Hepeating," *The Guardian*, May 16, 2022, https://www.theguardian.com/lifeandstyle/2022/may/16/hepeating-manterrupting-mansplaining-men-repeating-women-taking-credit.

90 **"interrupted during oral arguments":** Tonja Jacobi and Dylan Schweers, "Justice, Interrupted: The Effect of Gender, Ideology, and Seniority at Supreme Court Oral Arguments," *Virginia Law Review* 103 (2017): 1379; Tonja Jacobi and Matthew Sag, "Supreme Court Interruptions and Interventions: The Changing Role of the Chief Justice," *Boston University Law Review* 103 (2023): 1741.

91 **"colleagues are much more sensitive":** Maya Yang, "Let Her Finish: Interruptions of Female Justices Led to New Supreme Court Rules," *The Guardian*, October 15, 2021, https://www.theguardian.com/law/2021/oct/15/us-supreme-court-female-justices-interruptions-sonia-sotomayor.

92 **"'high-involvement' conversation style":** Deborah Tannen, *Conversational Style: Analyzing Talk Among Friends* (Oxford: Oxford University Press, 2005), 40–42.

93 **"a way for them to receive feedback":** Rachel Schlund and Emily M. Zitek, "Algorithmic Versus Human Surveillance Leads to Lower Perceptions of Autonomy and Increased Resistance," *Communications Psychology*, June 6, 2024, https://www.nature.com/articles/s44271-024-00102-8.

93 **"implemented for developmental purposes":** James Dean, "More Complaints, Worse Performance When AI Monitors Work," *Cornell*

Chronicle, July 2, 2024, https://news.cornell.edu/stories/2024/07/more-complaints-worse-performance-when-ai-monitors-work.

Chapter 16

96 **"what do I like the *least*":** "Will AI Replace Me?," *Fixable* podcast, produced by TED, October 16, 2023, 19:19, https://www.ted.com/podcasts/fixable/will-ai-replace-me-w-aj-jacobs-transcript.

96 **"don't like the blank page":** Ibid., 1:18.

96 **"never have a blank page":** Ibid.

Chapter 17

100 **"interact more compassionately":** Gina Kolata, "When Doctors Use a Chatbot to Improve Their Bedside Manner," *The New York Times*, June 12, 2023, https://www.nytimes.com/2023/06/12/health/doctors-chatgpt-artificial-intelligence.html.

101 **"took ChatGPT just minutes":** Ibid.

101 **"insurer granted the request":** Ibid.

101 **"similarly impressed":** Ibid.

101 **"gave him the words":** Ibid.

101 **"doctor is using a chatbot":** Ibid.

102 **"physicians are using this [technology]":** Ibid.

102 **"Similar concerns":** Keith Robert Fisher, "ABA Ethics Opinion on Generative AI Offers Useful Framework," American Bar Association, October 3, 2024, https://www.americanbar.org/groups/business_law/resources/business-law-today/2024-october/aba-ethics-opinion-generative-ai-offers-useful-framework/.

Chapter 18

104 **"increasingly turning to AI":** Rashi Shrivastava, "AI-Generated Employee Handbooks Are Causing Mayhem at the Companies That Use Them," *Forbes*, May 8, 2024, https://www.forbes.com/sites/rashishrivastava/2024/05/08/ai-generated-employee-handbooks-are-causing-mayhem-at-the-companies-that-use-them/.

104 **"generate their company handbook":** Ibid.

105 **"produce a severance agreement":** Ibid.

105 **"If your work is actually meaningful":** "Med-PaLM or Facepalm? A Second Opinion on LLMs in Healthcare," *Mystery AI Hype Theatre 3000* podcast, produced by DAIR Institute, August 28, 2023, 56:10, https://www.buzzsprout.com/2126417/episodes/13675879-episode-16-med-palm-or-facepalm-a-second-opinion-on-llms-in-healthcare-feat-roxana-daneshjou-august-28-2023.

105 **"scatterbrained employee":** Daniel Kotajlo et al., *AI 2027* (AI Futures Project, April 2025), 6, https://ai-2027.com/ai-2027.pdf.

105 **"No one's proofreading them":** Shrivastava, "AI-Generated Employee Handbooks."

Chapter 19

108 **"boring and repetitive tasks":** Nan Jia et al., "When and How Artificial Intelligence Augments Employee Creativity," *Academy of Management Journal* 67 (2024): 5.

108 **"allow us to outsource":** "What Is the Future of AI?," *AI in Focus*, produced by Knowledge at Wharton, YouTube, November 10, 2023, 12:44, https://www.youtube.com/watch?v=HNqtxT68l3Y.

109 **"biggest boost in productivity":** Ibid.

109 **"I came up with the idea":** *People I (Mostly) Admire*, produced by Freakonomics.

109 **"Levitt will tell you":** Stephen J. Dubner, "The Probability That a Real-Estate Agent Is Cheating You (and Other Riddles of Modern Life)," *The New York Times*, August 3, 2003, https://www.nytimes.com/2003/08/03/magazine/probability-that-real-estate-agent-cheating-you-other-riddles-modern-life.html.

110 **"I ended up delegating":** *People I (Mostly) Admire*.

110 **"work would be taken away":** "Why AI Is a Threat to Artists," *Tech Won't Save Us* podcast, June 29, 2023, 9:00, https://www.techwontsave.us/episode/174_why_ai_is_a_threat_to_artists_w_molly_crabapple.

110 **"old system involved caseworkers":** Virginia Eubanks, *Automating Inequality: How High-Tech Tools Profile, Police, and Punish the Poor* (New York: St. Martin's Press, 2018).

111 **"technology is no substitute for justice":** Liza Featherstone, "How Big Data Is 'Automating Inequality,'" *The New York Times*, May 4, 2018,

https://www.nytimes.com/2018/05/04/books/review/automating-inequality-virginia-eubanks.html.

Chapter 20

114 **"neglect the right things":** Oliver Burkeman, *Four Thousand Weeks: Time Management for Mortals* (New York: Farrar, Straus and Giroux, 2021), 72.

114 **"average human lifespan":** Ibid., 3, 234.

Chapter 21

118 **"delegating away what I loved":** *People I (Mostly) Admire*, produced by Freakonomics.

118 **"produce more but understand less":** Lisa Messeri and M. J. Crockett, "Artificial Intelligence and Illusions of Understanding in Scientific Research," *Nature* 627 (2024): 49.

118 **"really excited about its potential":** Jennifer Ouellette, "Producing More but Understanding Less: The Risks of AI for Scientific Research," *Ars Technica*, March 6, 2024, https://arstechnica.com/science/2024/03/producing-more-but-understanding-less-the-risks-of-ai-for-scientific-research/.

118 **"AI-assisted research":** Messeri and Crockett, "Artificial Intelligence," 53.

119 **"vulnerable to error":** Ibid.

119 **"tainted by the AI's influence":** Ethan Mollick, *Co-Intelligence: Living and Working with AI* (New York: Portfolio, 2024), 118–19.

120 **"an opportunity to engage deeply":** Salman Khan, *Brave New Words: How AI Will Revolutionize Education (and Why That's a Good Thing)* (New York: Viking, 2024).

120 **"Generative AI is best":** Dan Meyer, "Generative AI Is Best at Something," Dan Meyer Substack, February 20, 2024, https://danmeyer.substack.com/p/generative-ai-is-best-at-something.

121 **"The larger issue here":** Ibid.

Chapter 22

124 **"When I talk to people":** Helen Toner, "How to Govern AI—Even If It's Hard to Predict," TED Talk, YouTube, May 2024, https://www.youtube.com/watch?v-LUn8IjZKBPg.

124 **"a strange set of affairs":** Ibid.

124 **"AI can be confusing":** Ibid.

124 **"those building the technology":** Ibid.

Chapter 23

128 **"An improbable nightmare":** Louise Amoore, "Why 'Ditch the Algorithm' Is the Future of Political Protest," *The Guardian*, August 19, 2020, https://www.theguardian.com/commentisfree/2020/aug/19/ditch-the-algorithm-generation-students-a-levels-politics.

129 **"without a critical audience":** Daan Kolkman, "'F**k the Algorithm'? What the World Can Learn from the UK's A-Level Grading Fiasco," *LSE Impact Blog*, August 26, 2020, https://blogs.lse.ac.uk/impactofsocialsciences/2020/08/26/fk-the-algorithm-what-the-world-can-learn-from-the-uks-a-level-grading-fiasco/.

130 **"public officials everywhere":** Ibid.

Chapter 24

132 **"the A-Level scandal":** Tom Simonite, "Meet the Secret Algorithm That's Keeping Students Out of College," *Wired*, July 10, 2020, https://www.wired.com/story/algorithm-set-students-grades-altered-futures/.

132 **"I've talked to hundreds of people":** Rumman Chowdhury, "Your Right to Repair AI Systems," TED Talk, YouTube, June 5, 2024, https://www.youtube.com/watch?v=PxE0TWcT-kA.

132 **"know that their data is harvested":** Ibid.

133 **"the sphere of self-confidence":** Salman Khan, *Brave New Words: How AI Will Revolutionize Education (and Why That's a Good Thing)* (New York: Viking, 2024), 91.

133 **"Buffington has seen these gains":** Ibid.

133 **"Incoming high-school senior":** Sara Randazzo, "That Essay Got a B+. An AI Bot Graded It," *Wall Street Journal*, July 2, 2024, https://www.wsj.com/tech/ai/ai-tools-grading-teachers-students-396c2bfc.

134 **"ultimate human growth hormone":** Julie Lythcott-Haims, *Your Turn: How to Be an Adult* (New York: Henry Holt, 2021), 38.

135 **"discover and prioritize the core message":** Elyse L. Aurbach et al., "Half-Life Your Message: A Quick, Flexible Tool for Message Discovery," *Science Communication* 40, no. 5 (2018): 669–77, https://doi.org/10.1177/1075547018781917.

138 **"elegant economy of his communication style":** Stephen Budiansky, *Oliver Wendell Holmes: A Life in War, Law, and Ideas* (New York: W. W. Norton, 2019), 293.

139 **"freshness of his prose":** Ibid.

Chapter 25

144 **"sometimes it fails badly":** Arvind Narayanan and Sayash Kapoor, "ChatGPT Is a Bullshit Generator. But It Can Still Be Amazingly Useful," AI As Normal Technology. December 6, 2022, https://www.normaltech.ai/p/chatgpt-is-a-bullshit-generator-but.

145 **"you're too close to your own work":** George Saunders and Adam Grant, "The Art of Rough Drafts," *ReThinking with Adam Grant* podcast, October 31, 2023, https://www.ted.com/podcasts/rethinking-with-adam-grant/the-art-of-rough-drafts-with-george-saunders-transcript.

145 **"when a reader has a problem":** Haruki Murakami, *Novelist as a Vocation*, trans. Philip Gabriel and Ted Goossen (New York: Alfred A. Knopf, 2022), 100.

145 **"Whichever course I have followed":** Ibid., 100.

Chapter 26

150 **"College student Benjamin Craver":** Joseph Pisani, "The Student Who Was Suspended for a Prizewinning AI Tool Fights Back," *Wall Street Journal*, May 25, 2024, https://www.wsj.com/us-news/education/emory-university-suspends-students-eightball-ai-tool-3c0525cd.

151 **"designed to help students study":** Ibid.

152 **"historical neck broken":** Henry Adams, *The Education of Henry Adams* (1907; Project Gutenberg, 2013), https://www.gutenberg.org/files/2044/2044-h/2044-h.htm.

152 **"The year 1900":** Ibid.

153 **"the term 'knowledge worker'":** Peter Drucker, *The Landmarks of Tomorrow* (New York: Harper and Row, 1959), 93.

153 **"today's technological explosion":** Peter F. Drucker, "The First Technological Revolution and Its Lessons," *Technology and Culture* 7 (1966): 143.